More praise for
*How to Get Your Cat
To Do What You Want*

"Warren Eckstein is a Leo Buscaglia of the pet set. . . . The book is filled with many simple solutions for such common cat problems as scratching, clawing, and litter box mistakes, but his message is broader."

—*San Francisco Chronicle*

"Written in an easily read format, the short chapters deal not only with the usual care, feeding, and training information, but also with feline mental health issues of depression, midlife crisis, and stress. . . . Not a cold, clinical manual, this book gets no more cutesy than referring to cats as Kitty, he or she, and furball. It refers to them as dignified beings."

—*Albuquerque Journal*

"I would like to see this book made available to all current and prospective cat owners, for required reading."

—*Cat World International*

Books by Warren Eckstein

How to Get Your Cat to Do What You Want
(with Fay Eckstein)

How to Get Your Dog to Do What You Want

The Illustrated Cat's Life

The Illustrated Dog's Life

HOW TO GET YOUR CAT TO DO WHAT YOU WANT

Warren Eckstein and Fay Eckstein

FAWCETT BOOKS • NEW YORK

A Fawcett Book
Published by The Random House Publishing Group

Copyright © 1990 by Warren Eckstein and Fay Eckstein

Published in the United States by Fawcett Books, an imprint of
The Random House Publishing Group, a division of Random
House, Inc., New York, and simultaneously in Canada by
Random House of Canada Limited, Toronto.

Fawcett Books and colophon are trademarks
of Random House, Inc.

www.ballantinebooks.com

Library of Congress Catalog Card Number: 96-96719

ISBN: 0-449-91228-0

This edition published by arrangement with Villard Books, a division of Random House, Inc. Villard Books is a registered trademark of Random House, Inc.

Manufactured in the United States of America

First Ballantine Books Mass Market Edition: August 1991
First Ballantine Books Trade Edition: August 1996

15 17 19 18 16

To S.C. and M.C. for showing us the way;
D. Dee for all the times he made us laugh;
and our families, Charles and Ruth Eckstein,
Arzie, Linda and Sharon Schwartz,
for all their love and devotion, past and present

"In the beginning, God created man, but seeing him so feeble, He gave him the cat."
—Warren Eckstein and Fay Eckstein

CONTENTS

ACKNOWLEDGMENTS

We would like to thank our 40,000-plus pet clients and their owners. And a big special thank-you to Sharon Ann Schwartz for endless hours of proofreading.

Important Notes

In order not to insult any of my feline friends, you'll find throughout this book I switch back and forth from "he" to "she" and "him" to "her." Clearly it would have been easier to refer to Kitty as "it" and avoid this gender dilemma altogether. But I couldn't do that. Cats aren't "its." They're much too special for such a cold, nondescriptive label. So in the interest of fair play, for this book sometimes Kitty is a boy and sometimes Kitty is a girl. I hope I've given them equal time.

The Ecksteins believe in using lots of praise, love, hugs and kisses. Be sure your cat is declared healthy by the vet and isn't the type that might become frightened or aggressive or scratch or bite when suddenly showered with smooches or affection. Some cats react strangely when people are extra close.

The Ecksteins encourage you to read the entire book before trying any of their advice.

❀   ❀   ❀

INTRODUCTION

To own a cat is to understand the concept of living with a being of higher intelligence. Not amused by telephones, bills, and the mundaneness of everyday life, cats spend their entire day deciding on ways to improve their living conditions.

People don't choose cats, cats choose the people with whom they wish to live. When I hear someone say, "I hate cats," I don't frown or view them with disdain. I simply recognize that they haven't had the opportunity to be accepted and owned by a cat.

And how do you know when you've been picked to be owned by a cat? That's easy. He tells you.

My cat Mowdy certainly did. In fact, Mowdy added a new dimension to the art of conversation. He showed me that a little *simple* conversation wasn't enough. You see, cats have the capacity for well-thought-out discussions (and actions)—they just pick and choose on whom they want to use it. They outsmart us all the time.

Because I appear frequently on television and radio, manufacturers constantly send me the latest toys and gourmet foods for pets, hoping that after I try them out on my four-legged menagerie, I might mention them during one of my media appearances. So even though Mowdy had thirty thousand other people in my town to choose from, he knew that moving into my house was like moving into Kitty Disney World.

And that's what he decided to do—move in. One day, popping up out of nowhere, Mowdy simply strolled into my life. Well, he didn't actually stroll in—what he did was fuss and scream, so much so that he didn't give me much of a chance to decline his decision to relocate. I have an office in my house and Mowdy, who was unnamed and homeless at the time, positioned himself ever so cleverly atop my neighbor's car— which has a bird's-eye view through my office window— putting him in the perfect place to stare me down while I was on the phone. Mowdy looked me square in the eyes and started meowing. Not just any type of meow, mind you—but short ones, long ones, and many of different octave ranges. I'm sure some of his vocalizations were clearly audible to the entire neighborhood—if not the entire eastern seaboard. It was clear that Mowdy was carrying on a full-length conversation with me. I could hear it in his voice, and I could certainly see it on his face.

I'm embarrassed to say that I did not take Mowdy too seriously. I was already the proud owner of too many pets. As a matter of fact, I had recently gone into debt to buy a second home, a farm in upstate New York, not for me but for my pets; my animals needed a country home. There's only so much time you can hide a pet pig who weighs over one thousand pounds in a residential Long Island neighborhood. Sure, at first I passed him off as a very rare breed of dog. But it was easy then because he was small and I had taught him, like all my pets, to walk on a leash and harness. But with a pig there comes a point where you just can't fool people anymore. So I packed up my favorite little porker, whose name was Spotty, twenty-two rabbits, my ducks and chickens (all of whom have names and are pets), the various assorted abandoned dogs and cats I had taken in from the streets, and off we went to find them a new home of their own.

But it wasn't just our overcrowded feeling that caused me to ignore the talking feline. I assumed Mowdy had to be owned by someone in the neighborhood. He looked well fed, had a glossy coat, and seemed to be in tip-top physical condition. So because Mowdy didn't look needy—and because there comes a point in even the most caring animal lover's life when you just have to say "I have enough pets"—I tried to ignore him. But, the operative word here is *tried*—for there was no ignoring Mowdy. When I paid no further attention to him, he shifted gears and attacked my front door. It was as if Rambo had been giving this cat private lessons. Mowdy figured out a way to unclip the screen from the door, then managed to jump in, dumping himself between the screen door and the front door. Of course, he was stuck—or so he pretended. Personally, I don't think this particular kitty could ever get himself into anything he couldn't figure his way out of. But ear-shattering meows were now echoing through the entire house. Then the meows became screams. I ran to the door fully expecting to see some sort of catastrophe. But the very instant I opened the main door, *plop!*—Mowdy landed on his feet in the most regal manner and simply strolled into the living room. His mission was accomplished.

He had tried to tell me but I, being less intelligent, hadn't listened. So he had *showed* me. He had gotten me to do what *he* wanted.

I firmly believe that your cat is a member of your family. If you keep that in mind, if you truly feel it, your cat will act like one. That's one of the basic premises of this book. It's the best way I know to get your cat to do what *you* want.

Okay. Once you accept that premise, we've got to decide exactly how to treat the new family member.

It's really fairly simple—and the rest of this book is devoted to telling you just this: If you treat your cat with love, if you treat your cat with respect, if you treat your cat as if he or she is an intelligent, thinking animal, capable of making decisions, your cat will respond in positive, astonishing ways.

Can you talk to your cat and have her talk back to you? Yes. Can you get your cat to sit and stay and come and do other things that are normally considered impossible for a cat to do? Absolutely.

But first you've got to understand not only *that* a cat thinks, but *how* and *what* he or she thinks.

Then—and only then—will you be able to get your cat to do what you want.

And you know what? By the time you reach that point, your kitty is going to want to do the same things you want him or her to do. Not 100% of the time, of course. Nobody's perfect. But remember: part of the joy of having a cat is the joy of being around a freethinker. We don't want to turn Kitty into a robot, just into an intelligent and loving member of the family.

❧　　❧　　❧

HOW TO
GET YOUR CAT
TO DO
WHAT YOU WANT

❧　　❧　　❧

1

* * *

NEW-AGE THINKING
ABOUT CATS

RING OUT THE OLD,
RING IN THE NEW

Johnny Carson has proclaimed for years that cats do nothing but curl up on top of the television set where it's nice and warm, lay in the sun, or wait to be fed. Carson likes dogs and here's Johnny's reasoning—dogs *do* things! They come when called, fetch, and are actually happy to see you when you come home. On the other hand, he says, when you throw something for a cat to fetch he looks at you and as much as says, "Hey, go fetch it yourself." Then there's that joke that's been making its way around dog shows and newspaper columns about the difference between dogs and cats that says: "Dogs come when they're called, cats take a message and get back to you."

Cats have taken a bad rap for decades, but is their reputation deserved? When so many of the same types of comments keep popping up, don't you have to agree that there must be *some* degree of truth to it? Can so many people be wrong? You need only listen to any hard-core group of dog owners to find out the advantages of dogs over cats. But, when it comes to dog and cat owners discussing the excellence of each animal, be prepared for some hot and heavy debates; I've even seen a few that bordered on fistfights.

If you think I'm exaggerating, try this at the office tomor-

1

row. Gather a few dog and cat owners around the water cooler and toss out this question for discussion: "What makes the best pet—a cat or a dog?" At first there will be a few cute remarks, like "The only thing a cat can do if you're being robbed is to ask the burglar to feed it." Then I bet there will be a few examples of feline vs. canine behavior: "Dogs stay in the kitchen with you because they love being with you, but cats just hang out there because warm air blows in from under the refrigerator." I guarantee that in almost every case, there will be one dog and one cat owner who will begin to take the whole thing very personally, defending the pet of their choice. It will be a fight that would make Muhammad Ali proud. Just watch the fur fly.

THE BIG MISTAKE—
UNRAVELING THE MYSTERY

"Dogs are smarter than cats." "Dogs are better pets than cats." "Dogs are more affectionate than cats." "Cats are aloof and independent." I'm sick and tired of hearing all this non-sense and I'm not going to take it anymore. You shouldn't either.

Let's get one thing straight once and for all: *Any pet is a product of what's been put into him or her.* Two factors—and two factors only—determine the personality, intelligence, and overall disposition of a pet: (1) breeding—that both mates were genetically well-suited for each other, producing strong, healthy offspring or, in the case of a randomly bred stray, whether the odds were with the pet, so that the pet is physically sound, without inbreeding or any other genetic disorders—and (2) the environment in which the pet lives—what the owner does or does not do with that pet.

Notice I keep saying pet, not cat or dog. These two factors hold true for either a cat or a dog. But herein lies the mystery, because if what I say is true, then why do so many cats behave differently than dogs? Why are many cats so frightened when guests come over that they hide under the bed or in the closet? Why do so many *not* come when they're called? Why do cats look up at you and say, "Me? Are you talking to me?" and then turn around and walk off in the opposite direction?

Many cat owners often make one huge mistake, which interferes with proper cat rearing more than any other factor: *Because we have been brainwashed into thinking that cats are independent, aloof, sometimes less affectionate and certainly less trainable, many cat owners treat their cats differently just because they're cats!* We've heard these things so many times, we believe them to be true—and we raise our cats accordingly. If they don't respond to training, we simply don't follow through or, worse, don't try at all. The thinking often runs along the lines of "Hey, it's a cat, right? Cats can't be trained so why put in the effort?" Nothing could be further from the truth.

I BELIEVE CATS ARE SO SMART, THEY'VE CONVINCED PEOPLE THEY CAN'T BE TRAINED!

I remember when Mowdy first plopped himself down on the living room floor after cleverly removing the screen from the door. He acted as if he couldn't understand a thing except, of course, where he would lay his precious little head at naptime and how often he could con me into fixing extra meals. But Mowdy didn't stand a chance of fooling me. He had already tipped me off that he was one of God's clever creatures. Any cat that can disassemble my front door to let himself in can't be stupid. I'm embarrassed to admit I wasn't able to get that screen out for over a year. You may have guessed that I'm no whiz with a screwdriver and I suffered through one very long, cold winter. But for Mowdy it was no problem. He did it in minutes.

Due to their high level of intelligence, and their great natural instinct, our cats have outwitted many of us. When Kitty acts independent, she knows we'll get off her case and leave her alone, allowing her to pick and choose only those things she wants to do. I don't see the mystery in this. Exceptionally smart kids do the same thing all the time.

Now don't misunderstand me: If you're perfectly happy with your cat's behavior *and* she is happy and well adjusted, I'm not suggesting that you take her shopping for school clothes and throw her headfirst into an educational program just for the heck of it. Certainly I'm not suggesting that you torment and embarrass your cat by forcing her to perform stupid, silly tricks she doesn't enjoy.

What I am saying is that too many cats are living empty lives within the same four walls each and every day, 365 days a year. You can see it in their eyes. Some look vacant and empty, the result of no one having taught them anything. Too many cats are frightened and antisocial, diving under the bed the instant they hear the doorbell ring and they don't dare peek out until they're certain all intruders are gone for good. Others are so traumatized by trips to the veterinarian, that upon returning home they're shell shocked and disappear for days, hiding in dark, secretive places until the trauma wears off. Some cats behave so poorly at the vet's office that many owners actually choose not to bring their cats to the doctor except in extreme emergencies or when critically ill. Mowdy, on the other hand, appreciates challenges. He marches right into that vet's office and says, "Doc, here I am, make my day!" None of that squirming, screeching behavior from my boy.

KITTY'S BILL OF RIGHTS AND
THE FELINE FREEDOM MARCH

Cats have a right to a better life, free of emotionally crippling phobias. They have a right to be happy and well adjusted, not reclusive and scared, doing nothing but watching TV and hanging out in the window for the rest of their lives. They have a right to get out of the house, and not only for a possibly offensive trip to the vet's office. If you disagree, then why not have a caged, exotic animal for a pet? Just as most of us find offensive the thought of one of the big cats, like a beautiful cougar or tiger, locked in a pen for life, the type of ownership that many cats live through amounts to almost the same thing. The space may be bigger but the concept is the same.

What type of life are we providing for the cat that never leaves home? Just how fair are we being? Can we reasonably expect our cats to sit around and watch *General Hospital* and all the other soaps day in and day out? Just what is the cat supposed to do once he knows the answers to all the questions on *Jeopardy?* How should Kitty occupy himself when he already knows what Vanna will wear tonight?

Cats should have certain civil rights—and the number one right must be their proper education. Education ensures a reasonable life worthy of a cat's intelligence, instinct, and friendship. If we're going to keep any animal as a pet it must be done with a certain degree of dignity. Since we are the ones who have changed the terms of a cat's existence, it is up to us to further enhance our understanding of the cat and to guarantee a better feline life—not one spent hiding under beds or sentenced to serve a life term within the same four walls. Loving, feline friends deserve better treatment. We've created a number of problems for our domesticated cats and we must make it our responsibility to work through the strangling effects of their domestication.

Much of what you'll read in this book are totally new concepts about a cat's ability and need to learn, and what constitutes fair and responsible cat ownership. Some of these ideas will go against the grain of cat traditionalists. But I say, "Let's be fair!" Now, more than ever, we know just how intelligent cats are—and if we're going to keep them as pets, we must be concerned for their total welfare and fulfillment. Letting them rot at home day in and day out—doing nothing but sunning in the window, wishing that life held more for them as they vacantly stare out the window—is absolutely unjust. And anyway, Mowdy would never let me get away with it!

KITTY NEEDS STIMULATION

Years ago many of us lived in more rural environments, full of green places and almost free from the threat of vehicular traffic. Kitty could romp and play and you could watch her from the kitchen window as she maneuvered herself in and out of all sorts of playful jams. Sally, one of my previously owned strays, would tear around the yard at race-car speeds. Then in a flash he'd charge up the gigantic willow tree, coming to land on the remains of an old limb, a good fifteen feet up in the air. Sally, who by the way turned out to be Sal, a boy cat, although we never could quite bring ourselves to call him Sal, would look around with the most comical face, as if to say, "Okay, how did I get here, and now that I'm here would somebody pleeeease get me down off this thing."

That was in the old days. Today, much of suburbia is made of concrete and full of automobile congestion. Most cats, for their own safety, just can't roam free. If kitties are allowed to wander, owners run the risk of an accident-related, premature death. Those owners are able to say, I suppose, that at least the death came as the result of an exciting life, full of exploration and kitty adventure. This choice recognizes that the quality of an indoor life leaves something to be desired. Denying their cats the opportunity to be real cats is something these owners just can't tolerate. Good for them, I say, for understanding that cats need a better life—but I also say they should be strung up from the nearest oak tree for exposing their cats to a possible death under four wheels!

Yes, of course cats are bright and intelligent and have real needs; needs that require titillating life experiences and new areas to explore, smell, and even claw. Nature intended the cat to have certain inalienable rights, but man and the environment he has created have changed the game plan. And yes, certainly it's up to us to do something about it. We must help the cat adapt to a future that will salvage his dignity and offer some form of freedom—but without threatening his existence.

It's our obligation to ensure that Kitty's existence consists of more than running in for the can opener, lounging around after a meal, getting a little hugging and some loving before you leave or after you come home from the office, and a little brushing from time to time. This just isn't enough. If cats could revolt they would—*and they are!* They want their cake and they want to eat it, too. And you know what? Why shouldn't they?! There's a clever mind in that little furry body, one that has survived thousands of years—and not by accident! Kitty's boring life is one of the main reasons owners are experiencing so many behavioral problems with their furry friends. Never before has there been such a high incidence of troubled cats, creating a need for cat experts like myself and books like this. It's not just that now there are more cats around, but that the percentage of troubled, problem cats has risen dramatically.

My practice includes treating the psychological and behavioral problems of all sorts of animals: birds, llamas, goats, pigs, horses, and virtually everything else you can think of that has come my way over the years. But a large part of my interest is focused on cats and dogs; they mean so much to so many people. Lately, my office phone has been ringing off the hook with cat problems and my mail has been filled with letters about cats. Most of the problems boil down to cats that are living out most of their lives in the same home, within the same four walls, every day of the year, year in and year out. And the result is often a negative change in behavior.

To illustrate this point, I'd like to tell you about a snake I was called in to help. I know, I know, you're asking yourself what could a snake story have to do with your cat—but trust me, it does.

One day the owner of this boa constrictor, whose name was Sam, called me. He was worried because Sam had begun to act peculiar, so I went out to see them the next day. After checking out the situation, which, because it was so obvious, took all of two seconds, I declared, "Your snake's depressed. Your boa is bored!" Well you could have knocked over that owner with a feather. "Depressed!" he cried out. I didn't know if he was going to hit me or keel over laughing, so I figured I'd better start explaining.

"Sam's been in this same tank since you got him. He was only a foot long then, but now he's three feet and he's had it. It's the same old tank, decorated with the same old furniture. The same rock has been there since the beginning and so has the same tree branch. If you were that snake, wouldn't *you* be bored out of your mind by now?" And to underscore the point, I told him how darned lucky he was that Sam was still a sweet snake and that if he didn't do something about Sam's mental stimulation—and do it pretty soon—Sam the Sweety could easily turn into Sam the Snot-Nosed Snake. Too much confinement can make *any* animal aggressive.

The solution for Sam was easy—a bigger tank. He just loved his new spacious quarters and its new decorating theme— rocks, tree limbs and driftwood, all of which could be moved around and even easily replaced periodically. He was in snake heaven. He could slither and wrap himself around things to his heart's content. His depression days were over and there was an immediate, noticeable difference in his behavior as he rubbed against—and crawled up, around, and through—all his new stuff.

I think almost everyone will agree that cats are more intelligent and sensitive than Sam the snake. So if a snake can run into emotional and behavioral problems by having to live out a routine, humdrum existence, then certainly Kitty is capable of suffering from the same fate. *And you've got to do something about it!*

A CAT'S SELF-IMAGE

Cats have a strange way of living up—or down—to the image you project for them. Give them high expectations for their own ability and they'll reach for the stars, trying to achieve them and please you. Downgrade their abilities, by constantly telling them how displeased you are with their behavior, and you'll rip apart their self-esteem, making it impossible for them to believe in you and, most of all, in themselves.

Kitty needs a good self-image if she's to attain the goals you set for her. I'm obviously not talking about Harvard or Yale or a seat on the stock exchange; I am talking about Kitty attaining the goals of good behavior—being socially well-adjusted and blending well into the family unit while also maintaining his or her own identity and psychological well-being. We take for granted these goals when everything is right with Kitty. It's the sort of thing you don't miss until it's not there.

It's easy to tamper with how a cat feels about itself. There are three ways. One is passive—it sort of takes place without anyone realizing it. I learned about this from Mowdy.

RIPPING APART KITTY'S SELF-IMAGE— WHAT *NOT* TO DO #1

One of the worst ways one can tamper with the way Kitty feels about herself can sneak into the relationship without your even realizing it. As I said earlier, when Mowdy first arrived on the scene I was quite adamant about not wanting another pet. I had way too many already and was probably breaking every zoning law on the books. On the other hand, I certainly wasn't going to leave him on the streets to fend for himself. Of course, he stayed—but I wasn't very happy about it. This was the first time I had ever felt this way. Up to this point there was always room for one more wandering stray, not only in my home but in my heart. But this time I made the offer of room and board and nothing else. I just couldn't allow myself to get attached to yet another animal—or so I thought.

Then one day I saw it. I saw it in his eyes. He knew! Mowdy, that independent, determined and hard-headed feline, had a look of real pain in his eyes. It wasn't a look of physical pain, but an emotional one of disbelief and emptiness, and I swear I saw his watery, tearful eyes. How did this little furball know that he was not wanted on Vermont Avenue? I will never forgive myself for projecting that feeling to him. It wasn't *his* fault that he was left homeless, one of God's forgotten little creatures. He certainly deserved better from me. Although I had intellectually understood that a cat needed a good self-image, it was only through Mowdy's tears that I really began to realize the degree to which this was true.

Cats have a real need to have their egos stroked, to be told they're good, to understand that they're loved. They need image and confidence building as much as we do. And they need a certain amount of self-esteem to behave well. They need to develop inner strength if they are to try something new or to learn to trust in you.

RIPPING APART KITTY'S SELF-IMAGE— WHAT *NOT* TO DO #2

Bad-mouthing Kitty and spreading gossip about her is the second way owners can rip apart Kitty's self-esteem and destroy her self-confidence, creating psychological problems where they never before existed. Cats are very astute and can sense a lot of what's going on around them. Many are so clever that they can even tell when you're speaking of them in unflattering terms to other people. They'll hide their heads in shame while you discuss their mistakes with the neighbors. I've often said if you can't say something nice about your cat, don't say anything at all. Believe me, they know! Some cats even get embarrassed. Watch their faces and you'll see exactly what they're picking up. They know what's going on!

I once had a client who did nothing but complain about his cat. ''Darn cat hair all over the place, darn smell of that darn cat food, darn smell of the litter box, darn this, darn that, darn cat.'' It was a bad situation, to say the least. The client was stressed out, with a lot of problems—trouble on the job, trouble with his ex-wife, and trouble with the IRS, which had finally caught up with him. Although I could certainly sympathize with him, I've never been truly compassionate toward people who take out their problems on their pets, even though too many owners do exactly that.

The cat was becoming catatonic, no pun intended. She was so used to being scolded and verbally abused that every time she saw the owner coming, her behavior, due to sheer fear, took a turn for the worse. Cookie didn't mean to run across the coffee table, knocking over everything as she scurried out of the way, but she couldn't help trying to escape as fast as possible when she saw her owner. After waking from her nap she also didn't mean to stay, frozen with fear, in his favorite armchair. She knew he wanted to sit in it, but her frightened, sleepy brain couldn't figure out what to do except sit there and hiss, swatting her owner as he tried to swat her out of the chair.

It got to the point where Cookie *did* mean it when she soiled all over his pillow and mattress late one night. After all, it started not to make any difference to her what she did, right or wrong—she was always hearing how rotten she was anyway. I'm reluctant to admit I greatly enjoyed the story of how the owner unknowingly slipped into bed, only to find himself in Cookie's new version of a litter box. I thought it only fitting that my client should get his due. But, unfortunately, there were no winners here. Both cat and owner lost.

What happened was that these two had set up a catch-22. My

client's berating behavior triggered off Cookie's incorrect conduct, and her poor responses caused my client to react in an even worse fashion. His growing dislike of Cookie was crystal clear to her, and the ongoing battle actually affected her psychological balance. She became increasingly skittish and unhappy. The more they went at it, the more out of control things became. Cookie became so accustomed to hearing "Bad cat, stupid cat, darn cat!" that she believed it. Everything she did seemed wrong, so as a result she did nothing right. The owner kept yelling and Cookie became submissive, then defensive, and slowly aggressive as she could take no more.

Was Cookie a bad cat? No, but she was caught up in a bad situation. No one was nurturing her or helping her develop a good self-image. Was Cookie in fact a good cat, a pretty cat, a nice cat? Yes she was—but nobody bothered to tell her.

RIPPING APART KITTY'S SELF-IMAGE—
WHAT *NOT* TO DO #3

The most common way of undermining Kitty's self-esteem occurs when cat owners get flooded with advice from well-intentioned friends—neighbors and relatives telling them to correct the cat for everything he does wrong. So these owners scold, yell, hit, step on back paws, pick the cat up by the scruff of the neck, force Kitty onto his back in a submissive position, squirt water pistols in his face, or stick his nose in whatever mess was made.

Dwell on the negatives long and often enough and you can actually help Kitty develop a negative behavioral pattern, whereby she gets so much attention for doing something wrong and, by comparison, so little attention for doing something right, she figures she might as well act badly. At least then she gets some attention, even though it's negative. Kids, you may know, sometimes do exactly the same thing.

For many cats, *no* is the first word they hear in the morning when they're demanding a feeding from owners who are stumbling to the coffee pot with half-open eyes. *No* is also the last word they hear at night when they try to sneak close and cuddle up on the pillow. A lot of kitties constantly hear the word *no* for a variety of indiscretions, and it's this constant barrage of *no, no, no!* that undermines their self-esteem.

It's easy to ruin a cat's confidence. Most undermining is a result of this old-fashioned thinking that Kitty should always be corrected. She hears *no* for jumping on the counter, *no* for eating the bagel and cream cheese, *no* for sitting in the sink, *no* for helping to navigate the car, and *no* for being the 3:00 A.M. alarm clock. Some cats hear the word *no* so often that they believe that *no* is actually their middle name. Life isn't fun in a world of things you're not allowed to do.

Educating our four-footed feline friends should be a pleasurable experience, not a horror story. Riker's Island and Sing Sing might have had hard labor and solitary confinement but this is no way to treat our special family pet members. Of course, cats will sometimes do the wrong thing, but that's how they learn—that's how we all learn. It's inevitable that they'll soil on the best carpet in the house (they seem to have an uncanny way of knowing just which one is the most expensive). And Kitty may conduct her own taste test on the blanket corners and carpet fringes. But they can only learn what you want them to do by experimenting. How many of us as kids learned that the stove was hot only after we touched it? When it burned our fingers, we wanted a little comfort from our moms, not to get smacked in the face for touching it—our pride and fingers hurt enough already. And so it is with the cat's pride when she sees she's upset the people that love her most.

Cats are unique in the amount of pride they maintain, both about themselves and their behavior. They are sensitive little creatures with emotions and confidence that can be eroded, and

they're fully capable of being embarrassed by their behavior—
and the behavior of their owners.

THE *NO* SYNDROME

It's time to forget about the old-style mentality of raising Kitty.
Right now I can hear a lot of you saying that this *No, no, no!*
syndrome could never happen to you. *You* would never be that
constantly corrective when your wonderful, adorable cat makes
a mistake. Well, you might be right, but a lot of owners un-
dermine their cat's self-esteem and pride to a lesser degree.
This type of erosion, when compounded over a period of years,
can create a drastic end result.

Think about this for a moment. What would you do if your
cat (1) left long, deep claw marks in your brand-new reclining
chair, (2) stole the chicken cutlets off the counter, and (3) had
an accident on the floor?

Regarding the first situation, I bet you'd bring her over to the
chair, show her what she did wrong, and give her a smack. Even
if it's not a hard smack, I bet over 50 percent of everyone reading
this would give the cat at least a little swat. In the second situation, I bet you'd bring her over to the counter area, tell her *no*,
and the same 50 percent plus of all readers would give her a little
swat. If you discovered the chicken cutlets were missing right
after you discovered the destroyed chair, I bet the swat would be
harder than what you'd ordinarily care to admit. And for number
three, the accident on the floor, you would probably bring her
over to the mess, ask "What did you do?" scold or hit her, and
maybe even rub her nose in it. If the accident happened right after
the discovery of the clawed chair and the missing cutlets, I bet
those swats would be getting harder.

Now let's review the answers. I'll bet that without your
realizing it, you're already a victim of the *no* syndrome of cat
training and behavior. After all, patience has its boundaries and
is not limitless. Well, it doesn't have to be this way. We can
love our cats into good behavior.

BUILDING KITTY'S SELF-CONFIDENCE—
YES IS THE WAY TO GO

The easiest way to create a confident cat that behaves well is to spend more than equal time on the things the cat does right. Sure Kitty gets plenty of corrections when he does caca, doo doo, pooh pooh where he's not supposed to—but do you spend the same or, better yet, more time kissing, hugging, and loving him when he uses the litter box or performs some other minor feat? I doubt it. Most people don't. At best there's a "good boy" and a pat on the head. But what happened to "Yeah! What a good boy!" followed by kisses, hugs, a belly scratch, a head rub, more kisses, extra hugs, and then "You're a terrific cat, wow are you a good boy!" followed by more kisses and hugs, another pat on the head and then, when you're done, repeating the whole process all over again?

Neighbors might find your antics a bit strange, but why would you care? Your cat will be well behaved, while they're struggling along for months or years with homes reeking like bad pet shops and full of tattered furniture. You'll always have the last laugh. I've even had people tell me their kids got potty trained at the same time they were working with Kitty because of all the praising and loving going on. Now *that's* a fringe benefit if ever I heard one.

You must present a clear picture for your cat of exactly what makes you happy. Cats usually don't have an opportunity to see this as clearly as we think they do. We all know that pets are willing to please their masters—so when they don't, don't you think it might be that their masters just aren't getting their points across? We don't have to dominate our cats with corrective techniques, we just have to go overboard on all the things our kitties do properly. Believe me, they do more good things than you probably realize, so we must take the time to constantly tell them how wonderful they are. We must love, kiss, hug, and touch them for every positive accomplishment. Cats that feel good about themselves will behave better for you. If you build their confidence they will respond in kind. They must have a good self-image. If they think they're a failure at life, then what's the sense of trying? Let them know how smart, intelligent, and well loved they are. They'll live up to your expectations.

And please don't reserve your positive thoughts and actions only to those times when Kitty has done something right. It's okay to tell her how wonderful she is for no reason at all. Stroke her ego and help her build a positive self-image. So go ahead, give Kitty a hug and a big kiss. Tell her what a good cat she is, even if she's doing nothing. Praise her, tell her she's wonderful, and give her a kiss and a hug for no reason. And while you're at it, give her a hug and a kiss for me.

DOES KITTY THINK?

I hope someone from up above will help me because I know I'm going to get myself in a lot of hot water with what I'm about to say. One of the most rip-roaring debates between myself and many clinically trained behaviorists and psychologists is over whether cats have the ability to think and make decisions. Many people who study animal behavior maintain that most animals don't think or make independent decisions. Instead, they believe that Kitty's responses are conditioned and in fact are ones we have helped to create. Some say that the extent of Kitty's response is to come running when she hears the can opener, since food almost always follows and we have conditioned her to this response. But you know what's so strange? When I'm hungry and I hear my wife in the kitchen using the can opener, I come running, too. Either I'm only as intelligent as my cat or my cat is as intelligent as I am—it depends on how you look at it. Some of these experts insist that only man is capable of putting one and one together and coming up with two, only man can assess a situation and think out what his response should be. Well, both Mowdy and I have learned to put one and one together when we hear the can opener and we both come running. Sometimes it's a race to the kitchen to see who can get there first. Mowdy usually beats me. He's learned the fine art of running between my legs in such a way that he won't get hurt, but I slow down or fall flat on my derriere. That cat outsmarts me all the time.

I believe that cats are very capable of applying their genius to an array of situations. Big exotic cats demonstrate their intelligence both in the wild and in captivity all the time. Most laymen don't seem to doubt that lions and tigers have a real intelligence of their own. Actress Tippi Hedren, who will be forever remembered for her legendary role in Alfred Hitchcock's *The Birds*, is a friend of mine. Tippi runs the Shambala Preserve in Acton, California, part of the Roar Foundation. She cares for, among other neglected creatures, lions and tigers that have been abused, mishandled, or are no longer wanted by zoos and circuses. It's a wonderful operation and I highly suggest that you include it in your itinerary if you live in or are traveling to southern California.

Tippi has daily contact with these big cats in a way that only a few people on earth have. She is the first to say that anyone who believes these animals can't think or don't possess real intelligence doesn't have nearly enough experience with them.

Tippi's book, *The Cats of Shambala*, contains pictures of her big cats (as well as her gorgeous daughter Melanie Griffith). Any animal behaviorist or trainer looking at these glorious photos can see that there's no way they could have been staged just for the camera. Big cats don't sleep in bed with you just to produce an interesting photograph, nor do they, for the same reason, ride in your car or boat, enter your home through the kitchen windows, join you at the dinner table and, most of all, hug you so close that you can see the love and affection just oozing out of them. Don't tell me these cats don't have intelligence. Don't try to tell Tippi Hedren that either!

On the smaller cat scale, no one conditioned Mowdy to bang

his dish relentlessly when feeding time was overdue. No one conditioned him to sneak onto the dining room table when I'm not around or to jump off as soon as he hears me approach. He knows it's not allowed—but since he wants to do it anyway, he'll wait until I'm out of the way. The second I return, I'll hear the thump from his leap off the table, and as I enter the room, I'll find him sitting on the floor, ever so angelically. He wasn't conditioned into this behavior. Sure he knows I don't like him up there, but I definitely didn't condition him to sneak up and know when to jump down just before I could catch him. Mowdy figured that out all on his own. He put two and two together and realized how he could outsmart his pop.

Now, before condemning me as some sort of ineffective problem solver, let me say that I could easily stop Mowdy from jumping up there. But since he has transformed himself into a basically well-behaved cat, I allow him a few indiscretions. We sort of play cat and mouse; he knows I don't like it, but he also knows I won't say anything unless he does. It's a good arrangement and it works for us.

David G. Myers's book *Psychology*, used in many college courses, defines classical conditioning as "a type of learning in which a neutral stimulus, after being paired with an unconditioned stimulus, begins to trigger a response similar to that normally triggered by the unconditioned stimulus (also known as Pavlovian or respondent conditioning)." Now even for those owners who have a lot of trouble getting past all those fancy words paired together, there's one word we've all come to know, and that's Pavlov. We all remember *Pavlov* from those dog-conditioning experiments we learned about in junior and senior high school, and it's those Pavlovian statements that always rub me the wrong way because they are always about animals being conditioned.

The same book defines intelligence as "the capacity for goal directed adaptive behavior (behavior that successfully meets challenges and achieves its aims). It involves the abilities to profit from experience, solve problems, reason, remember, and so forth.'' It seems to me that animals other than man are conspicuously left out of the definitions and examples of intelligence. Thinking and intelligence are most often described as examples of human behavior, while conditioning, much more frequently and sometimes exclusively, is applied to non-human animals.

My answer to this is that I wish some of the people with whom I do business were as intelligent as some of the cats I've met over the years—and I've worked with Fortune 500 executives, politicians, celebrities, and highly educated professionals. Believe me, there's a long list of people who should only hope to be half as intelligent as the average cat.

It's not that I disagree with the concept that many animals are conditioned in their behavior. It's just that I can't understand man's egotistical philosophy that only we are sufficiently intelligent to actually think and reason. I'll readily agree that humans, felines, canines, and so forth, are all conditioned in their responses as they go through life. However, if the scientists are adamant, insisting that only humans think and the rest of the animal kingdom is conditioned and dependent on instinct, then I'll do battle with them forever.

To illustrate this point I thought it would be interesting if we took one of these situations and assessed it from Kitty's perspective, seeing how she applies her intelligence. Can Kitty think? You be the judge.

Have you ever had to give a pill to your cat? Most owners have, as from time to time almost all kitties get sick and need some form of doctoring. Well, popping a pill into an animal's mouth is no big deal for me. I've always prided myself on my hands-on experience and consider myself different than many others in my field who write and lecture about pets and animals. Although they may have a genuine love and respect for animals, they are what I call animal advocates. There's certainly nothing wrong with that, but they often lack the experience of actually working with and educating cats while resolving behavioral problems and the like. These animal advocates are often well groomed, in suits and ties, with well-manicured fingernails as they make their television talk-show rounds. I, on the other hand, work daily with these animals, on my hands and knees at their level (all of my jeans have worn-out knees). Five minutes before any TV talk show, you can find me in the bathroom frantically trying to make my working hands look presentable for the television cameras. My sister-in-law has even gone so far as to buy me bunches of those white sticks you rub under your nails to make them look clean and less stained. When you *really* work with animals for a living you just never quite look like Barbie and Ken dolls.

Anyway, I've always prided myself on being able to pop a pill into the mouth of virtually any animal, particularly a domestic pet such as a cat. I know that a lot of novice cat owners who are reading this live in deadly fear of having to get a pill down Kitty's throat, but when you work with these animals professionally on a daily basis, it's no big deal. Well, the day finally came when Mowdy needed medication. With pill in hand I approached him, tilted back his head, popped in the pill, rubbed his throat a bit, and when I heard the appropriate swallow, got up from the floor and congratulated myself for a job well done. No sooner had I done this, when I heard the tiniest little *plop*. Looking down, there was the pill on the floor. Mowdy looked up at me and smiled, ever so sweetly, "Okay, so I must have missed. I'll just do it one more time," I said. Smart cats have a way of getting you to talk to yourself.

I picked up the pill and approached Mowdy for the second time. He didn't run, he didn't hide, and once again I tilted back his head, opened his mouth, popped in the pill, stroked his throat, waited for the gulp, and *voilà!* the pill was swallowed—or so I thought. *Plop!*—there it went again. This time he planted it squarely on top of my foot.

"Okay, okay," I told myself. "I'm not losing my touch.

I'm just not paying attention." I picked up what was now this disgusting, sticky little pill, tilted back Mowdy's head, put the pill in his mouth, and stroked his throat until I knew he *had* to have swallowed it. This time I checked his mouth very carefully. There was no pill to be found. I had succeeded. I was feeling much better. "That old cat can't outsmart me"—or so I thought.

Thirty minutes later there was Mowdy, tugging at my pants leg. He wanted to tell me something but I didn't quite catch what he was saying. I got up and started to walk around, giving Mowdy the opportunity to guide me to whatever it was he was trying to communicate. Well, he herded me into the living room and there, next to the loveseat, was this globby pile of something. I got closer to take a better look and there, right before my eyes, was . . . the pill. I looked at Mowdy and do you know what he did? He looked me smack-dab in the eyes and smiled—ever so sweetly.

Did Mowdy know exactly what he was doing? Did he figure out how to stash that pill somewhere in his mouth so even my close-up inspections couldn't unearth the pill? Did he grin and smile at me just to prove his point? You bet he did! Did I in any way, shape, or form condition Mowdy to go through that step-by-step procedure? You bet I didn't! Mowdy, the con man cat, figured out the whole thing all by himself.

I don't have to be convinced that cats have the ability to think things out and make decisions—I've seen it firsthand time and time again. I've even seen cats learn how to open doors—not just push them, mind you, but actually jump up on the door, turn the knob, and let themselves in. No one conditioned them to do this, but by observing and understanding that the knob mechanism was responsible for getting them into a room, they learned how to do it.

I've seen cats outsmart human beings plenty of times. Long-time cat owners have lots of stories about how their cats outmaneuvered them into getting what they wanted. (I know it's embarrassing to admit to being outsmarted by Kitty—but we're all friends here.) Cats have an amazing way of manipulating human beings. So don't tell me cats can't think. Don't tell me their behavior is only instinctive or conditioned. Don't bother. I'll never be convinced. I *know* cats think.

2

❧ ❧ ❧

IT'S OKAY TO TALK TO YOUR CAT

CAT CHATTING

I think most of us accept the concept that our cats do indeed talk to us. But it may be a little harder to convince you that your talking back to the cat is one of the most important things you can do to establish a strong relationship with your feline pal.

I must admit I feel a little nutty sitting here writing that it's okay to talk to your cat. But over the years I've both developed and stumbled upon a large number of skills that are breakthroughs in cat communication. Most of these skills can be learned by almost anyone willing to try—and I guarantee they will enhance whatever conversational tools have already been formed between you and your cat. So if you already talk to your cat and aren't ashamed of it, this book is definitely for you. And, by the way, you're in good company. My career in the pet behavior field has allowed me to work with some of the world's most famous people, and none of them hesitate to have a conversation with their cat. Beautiful Linda Evans, formerly Krystle Carrington of television's *Dynasty*, talks to her cat. Ron Reagan, Jr., told me he talks to his. TV's Golden Girls Betty White and Rue McClanahan also confessed to talking to their special four-footed friends. I've always found that the most sensitive, creative, and intelligent people don't hesitate to talk to their pets. Fashion designer Oleg Cassini confided to me that he talks to all his pets, which also happen to include miniature horses and a pet pig. First Lady Barbara Bush told me not only that she talks to her pets, but that some have actually slept in the presidential bed. So, like I said before, if you already talk to your little four-legged friend, you're in very good company.

There is, I'm sure, a category of owners who think talking to a cat is absurd. I can hear them grumbling now: "What am I supposed to say, 'How was your day at work, Kitty?' " If you're in this category I beg you not to put down this book, because there's so much you can learn. A wonderful, close relationship between you and your cat is just waiting to materialize. Read further and you'll see how a little education in talking with your cat can make your relationship very special.

There's a third category of cat owners to whom I want to appeal. They're the ones who lock the doors, pull down the shades, and then, when they're sure no one can hear, begin to chatter away to their cats. I call these people closet cat talkers. They do it all the time but it will be a cold day in you know where before they admit it in public. For those owners I'm telling you right here, right now: *It's okay to talk to your cat.* It's so okay, that you *should* be doing it and not feel the need to hide it. So, drag yourself out of the closet, and don't be ashamed or embarrassed. I know other people can make you feel insecure; you may even become the butt of friendly jokes. But ignore these nonbelievers! They're missing out by not opening up to the possibilities of communicating with animals. Just because they won't take off their blinders, don't let them stifle you. You wouldn't let them make fun of you for talking to your kids, would you?

OLD-FASHIONED PERCEPTIONS

It wasn't many years ago that cat-talking owners would have been considered the crazy people on the block. Even now, people with old-fashioned perceptions might still consider you on a par with the local lunatic if you discuss your problems with your feline friend. But there's no reason in the world not to have an extended conversation with your pet. Go ahead, talk about religion, politics, or the latest joke you heard at work. Many recent medical studies say you just might be better off if you and your pet get into a few heavy conversations. After all my years of being on the cat conversation bandwagon, the "prove it to me" scientists are finally agreeing that you could end up healthier, happier, and better adjusted emotionally if you talk to your fuzzy companion.

If discussing the Sunday *Times* isn't up your alley, at least tell Kitty he's a good guy, even if it's for no specific reason. If you're taking a walk and something interesting crosses your path, tell Kitty to look at it and ask him what he thinks. Okay, so passersby might think you're a little strange (all right, all right—make that a *lot* strange). But you'll build up Kitty's vocabulary and heighten his awareness of things around him.

Now let's back up for a moment. You probably got stuck on the sentence that talked about building up Kitty's vocabulary. Well, I believe cats have a rather large list of words they can understand. Don't be fooled by some experts who say the average cat comprehends, at best, ten or twenty words. When Mowdy moved in he knew none of the standard vocabulary. Today, through a little bit of Kitty conversation, he has developed some fine language skills, and his comprehensive skills run deep. He even understands and responds to the infamous command *come*, which cats *supposedly* can't learn.

Cats can understand a lot more than a few words—but only if you talk to them. Kitty can't learn the words just because you think about them. You have to say them and in such a way that Kitty knows you're talking to her. Take it from me, Kitty will try to understand what you're saying. Even the biggest doubting Thomases among you must have seen Kitty tilt her head from side to side, wrinkling up her little forehead as she tries to figure out what her human "mom" and "pop" are saying.

Or if Kitty isn't a brow wrinkler, then I bet she's a starer, watching ever so intently as you rant and rave about whatever ails you.

EXPANDING ON KITTY'S NATURAL LINES OF COMMUNICATION

All you have to do is take Kitty's brow wrinkling or staring one step further. Talk directly to her, like the real cat she is, not like some lump of Play-Doh on the floor. You'll get out of it what you put into it. Be an intelligent conversationalist and you'll develop an intelligent listener who'll learn to communicate and develop her own dialogue with you in a very special feline way.

Cats all over the world understand that their owners are leaving for the day when they get a kiss at the door and hear those famous words: "Now you be a good Kitty and take care of the house until Mommy and Daddy get home." You can see it in your cat's face that she's come to know what this means. It's her standard good-bye and she doesn't have to fret from separation anxiety—she *knows* you'll be home a little later because you told her so. You can almost hear Kitty say, "Sure Mom, sure Pop, no problem. I'll take care of things. I guarantee no mouse will even try to get near the place." Then off she'll go with a yawn, ready to embark on a morning snooze, content with the fact that you told her you'd be back. Okay, so you're a real skeptic and you say there's absolutely *no way* Kitty knew exactly what was said. Then at least consider that Kitty was reassured by your calm tone of voice that everything in her life was okay.

CATS CAN UNDERSTAND

Many of us say good-bye to our cats. We say good night before we go to sleep, we ask them if they're hungry, and we even ask them what's the matter if their little eyes are squinty and we suspect they're not feeling very well. Yes, many of us do these things, and subsequently—and not so amazingly—our cats begin to understand some basic vocabulary. Any animal that has the inherent intelligence to know when the refrigerator door is open, even if she's sleeping in a second-floor bedroom on the opposite end of the house and can get to the refrigerator faster than a speeding bullet, has the basic intelligence to comprehend not only simple words but more than a few complex thoughts as well. The question is: Does the little furball want to bother to understand you and, if so, does she want to let on that she understands? Once Kitty sends the right signals that she knows what you're saying, there's no turning back. Kitty's tipped her hand. No longer can she stand there and play dumb when you call her. No longer will she be able to force you to go to the cabinets and make you shake that food box in order to get her attention. Very clever, these cats of ours—don't underestimate them. They know what the deal is, but they won't let on unless you help them develop the art of conversation and make it worth their while. Hey, there are lots of husbands and wives who don't bother doing much talking and listening to each other, and look what happens to their marriages—they become stagnant and boring. You certainly don't want that to happen to your relationship. Why would you let it happen in your relationship with your cat?

Think about it from the cat's point of view. If all you heard was "Here, kitty, kitty, *psss, psss,*" you as a feline might say, "Big deal, why bother? I can get that from a stranger." But if you actually try to engage your cat in some real conversation, you're going to be surprised. But don't expect immediate results. There are no fast fixes for relationships that have become so boring that communication breaks down—be it between two people or between an owner and a cat. The longer you and your cat have been involved in a less than exciting relationship, the longer it's going to take to undo the damage. A few weeks probably won't make much of a difference. Give it a few months or more and you'll slowly find that Kitty will be ready to call some sort of truce to her attitude that "I'm just an independent, aloof cat and what could you possibly expect from me?"

You'll know when you've broken through. There will be more eye contact, more up close and personal cuddly situations, and more vocalizing. Listen hard and you'll learn the language. Those different vocalizations will mean something once you catch on to her lingo. Just keep listening. It's also important to let Kitty know you're trying to understand. Even if you haven't figured out how to translate what she's saying yet, she'll know if you're really making the attempt—and that's what counts. Think of it as a trip to France and you don't know a word except *oui*. It will be tough, but you'll get by. Both you and the Frenchmen will keep at it until you get your point across. As time goes by you'll learn the language, a little at a time. Even though things are rough around the edges, everyone's aware that communication is attempting to take place. Well, there's no difference here with Kitty.

Once Kitty understands the basic words, you can even give her a call when you're away from home and leave a message on the answering machine. Tell her you miss her. She'll hear it and know you still love her. That's what I do for my cat Mowdy and his dog pal, Tige.

If you don't talk to Kitty she can't learn. It's as simple as that. If you don't try and don't keep at it, you can't learn either. Just think of the Frenchmen. *Oui, oui.*

KITTYSPEAK—HOW YOUR CAT TALKS TO YOU

You don't have to be a pet psychic, if there really is such a thing, and you don't need special powers to interpret what Kitty says. I believe any owner, if sufficiently interested, can come to understand how Kitty speaks, as well as exactly what she is saying. It's easy and it doesn't require you to peer into the depths of the cat's brain with some mysterious power or sixth sense. You only have to learn how to translate the feline language.

Before I go any further I'd like to quickly make a point for nonbelievers in the "kitty can talk theory."

One of the best examples of feline language is nonverbal, but the message comes over loud and clear nonetheless. It's the one look most cat owners know and have already interpreted by themselves, with no help needed from me. It's the look you get when you ask Kitty to do something she doesn't want to do. First she puts her back to you, which in and of itself has its own translation, but as a matter of politeness I don't think we have to spell it out. We all know what it means when the end of the cat that doesn't have two ears and a cute nose gets flashed at you. Next, Kitty will usually follow up with a glance tossed in your direction that says, "Oh puh-lease, you've got to be kidding." At that point cat owners know they've lost. Kitty has spoken—and Kitty said "forget it."

For years humans have thought that among all the species, only *we* have a language that can be learned and only *we* can communicate with each other. Well, nothing could be further from the truth. Recently, much work has been done on the complex language of dolphins and porpoises; other studies have demonstrated much the same with gorillas. I believe that virtually every animal has a language of its own, including the highly intelligent cat. Learning how to understand the language of cats, or Kittyspeak, can bring the relationship between you and sweet Kitty to new heights.

Owners trying to learn Kittyspeak should remember that language isn't only the verbal transmission of actual words. In the case of cats it also includes various vocalizations and Kitty's nonverbal communication, the language of the body.

Hundreds of courses and special programs around the world

provide company executives and communication majors the opportunity to learn about human body language. A greater understanding of what a person is really saying can give you an edge both in the business world and in dealing with people in general. Things like: observing the eyes—do they make solid contact with the speaker's or do they dart around; does the person scratch his head, slouch in a chair, walk with stooped shoulders, cross his legs, cross her arms, squirm around a lot? These elements of human body language can tell you a lot about the person with whom you're doing business or simply carrying on a conversation.

Well, in adhering to my old philosophy that the human animal is not a whole lot different from or better than other animals, I profess the same sort of body language thinking about cats. If anything it's even of *more* importance since cats, in the wild or when left to their own devices, depend greatly on body language. They interpret the body language of other cats, and different animals as well, to find out their intentions and whether they're friend or foe. They rely on it for telling other felines what's on their mind.

Cats go one step further with body language. They watch people ever so closely. If your otherwise friendly cat takes an immediate dislike to someone, I suggest you take another look. I'd almost be willing to bet the house that Kitty's right. Too often, I've seen people who try to hide their malicious intent by vocalizing nice thoughts—but they can't fool my Mowdy. He sees through them.

Before you break out the Berlitz language course on Kitty-speak, it's important to recognize that each cat will have his or her own variation. While it's true that there are a number of fundamentals that remain unchanged from one cat to another, each Kitty will set her own tone and have the equivalent of her regional accent. It's best to explain the differences first in human terms. For example, a simple phrase like "That's great'' can mean very different things depending on who's saying it and for what reason. A happy-go-lucky, bubbly type person would be very sincere and positive when using the phrase, but someone who's a bit depressed or cynical might sneer and mean just the opposite indicating disdain by using the identical ''That's great.''

Individual cats may also have their own innuendos when communicating, and often those innuendos tend to be regional. Now, mind you, I'm not saying that Southern cats say ''Meow, y'all'' or that tough Brooklyn street cats say ''Yo—meow!'' What I am saying is that cats from different areas adapt some of the same attitudes as their human counterparts, affecting change in language and personality. Cats living in very hot climates tend to communicate at a slower pace, just like their owners. Their body language is more laid back; even their vocalizations may be slower in coming. Warm weather kitties tend to be more relaxed, just like the human animal. It's simply too hot to be quick in motion and spirit. On the other hand, cold weather urban cats are pretty quick to let you know what's going on. The cool weather and fast pace of the city doesn't allow them, or their owners, the luxury of a lot of free time to get their points across. A hot weather kitty might amble over to let you know it's time for food, while a cold weather cat could just about knock you down to let you know her internal dinner bell is ringing. At the other end of the spectrum there's the rural farm cat, who has developed all sorts of depth to his communication skills; there's just so much more to relate to as he bounces around in the open fields.

As I mentioned before, Kittyspeak takes two forms. To understand Kitty properly, you'll have to become fluent in both verbal and nonverbal language. To help you along, I've provided some easy tips in the next few sections. Eventually, you'll be able to understand just what Kitty is talking about and

how you can talk back to her. You *can* communicate with
Kitty—you just have to know how to go about it.

KITTYSPEAK CONTINUED— PURRING

I know all about purring. Mowdy has mastered all its forms—
from the highly adorable, barely audible purr to the one that
will rip out your eardrums. When Mowdy really wants to purr,
he purrs.

Purring is one sound all cat owners know. But, as with other
cat characteristics, the reason for purring—a sound that seems
so simple—is more complicated than you might think. What
makes a cat purr and what purring means are issues that cat
lovers have debated for centuries. To this day there are still
disagreements on the whys and wherefores of the purring experience. Once again little Kitty has confounded the experts.

WHY KITTY PURRS

There's been so much debate over the reasons why cats purr
that some people may have additional purring theories other
than mine. Although I think I've covered every theory known
to man, as I've said before, cats are truly very complex creatures and I've learned never to be too secure in my thinking that
I know every little thing about cats. That said, here we go—it's
purr time:

A purring cat is a happy cat.

A purring cat is a snoring cat.

A purring cat may be an upset cat.

A purring cat is a friendly cat.

A purring cat is acknowledging your friendship.

A purring cat can be an anxious cat.

A purring mother cat is allowing her newly born kittens to
feel the vibration of her purr. Tiny, defenseless, newborn kit-

tens, having no eyesight and poor senses of smell and hearing, use the vibrations from the mother's purring as a homing device.

A purring mother cat lets the little ones know that she's ready for nursing or that she's content while nursing.

On the other hand, a purring kitten lets the mother know that she's nursing successfully.

A purring cat may be in pain.

A purring cat is getting ready to take a snooze.

A purring cat may be an absolutely delighted cat.

And remember, there could be more reasons.

MY PURRING THEORY

While every expert has an explanation as to why Kitty purrs, I believe she purrs not for one reason alone, but for a variety of reasons. When combined with other factors and events taking place at the same time, purring may indicate Kitty's intent and exactly what she has on her mind at that very moment.

Although I don't dispute its validity in some cases, I'm not a big believer that most cats purr when upset, in pain, or during similarly negative experiences. I generally find that a purring cat is a happy cat, content with its surroundings. I do adhere to all the Mother Kitty and Baby Kitty reasons for purring; nature is amazing when it comes to allowing moms to care for their young. I also believe that purring is one of Kitty's signals to let us know that she cares and all is right between her and the world (or at least her owner). If you don't believe that one, pay attention to the following story.

Cheryl Tiegs, one of the most concerned and responsible pet owners I've ever met, is a client of mine. But this story is not really about her; it's about her executive assistant of many years, Barbara Shapiro. When I was working with Cheryl and her pets, Barbara was generally around and made no bones about not being one of the world's greatest pet enthusiasts. It wasn't that she didn't like them; she simply didn't have the time or inclination to have a pet. I wasn't concerned, since I knew it was just a matter of time before Cheryl and I converted her.

The big day arrived. The call to my office was from Barbara. "Guess what?" she said. "I've got a kitten!" And there was Barbara telling me all about the most adorable little kitty antics that were taking place in her household. "Never," she said, "could I have imagined that a cat could bring such fun into my life." Bingo, another Warren Eckstein pet-loving convert. My job was done.

But the continuing saga of the Barbara Shapiro story wasn't over yet. Before I could blink my eyes, another call came into my office. "Guess what?" she said. "I've got two *more* kittens and they're *all* great!" I was impressed. Within two shakes of a cat's tail, then there were four—three kitties and Barbara Shapiro.

Although Barbara had already learned to love those little kittens, there was one eventful day when it became crystal clear that her cats were truly special to her. That day, bad news about a friend reached her, at a time when she was particularly busy and tired. Upset about the news, she went to bed early that night and before she knew it she had company. She was surrounded. For the first time ever, all three of the Kitty Kids pounced on her, jumping into bed at the same time, cuddling up so very close and purring as if they knew she needed some comfort from her friends.

"How did they know and why were they purring?" she asked me, but she didn't need to hear my expert advice. In her heart Barbara knew the reasons. Cats aren't just animals with whom you share the house. They are caring, compassionate creatures. Sensing that Barbara was upset, her cats curled up as close as they could get and purred to let her know that just because everything wasn't right with the world, everything *was* right within their family. Barbara's cats offered their purring just for her. A special sound and a special closeness—just when she needed it most.

HOW KITTY PURRS—
THE BIG DEBATE

Experts don't agree on this one either. How cats purr has stirred up more controversy than perhaps any other point pertaining to felines. Three theories prevail.

- *False vocal cord theory:* Cats possess vocal cords as well as another set of cords commonly called false vocal cords, more correctly called vestibular folds. When air is inhaled and exhaled one false cord rubs against the other. Some experts believe this is the reason behind the purr.
- *Muscle contraction theory:* Some of the laryngeal muscles contract and cause a buildup of pressure.
- *Turbulent blood theory:* Turbulence is created when blood flow increases through the heart's main veins. It is the most turbulent when the main vein constricts as the blood passes through the chest area. The swirling blood is said to create the rushing, whirling sound which is amplified by the diaphragm. Some experts say that after traveling up the air passages and into the head area of the sinus and skull, the noise becomes purring.

Taking it one step further, some experts think that when a cat curls or arches its back the motion of the blood increases and so does Kitty's purr.

Taking it even another step further, other experts believe that the blood turbulence and purring increase when Kitty feels some form of emotion.

I believe that emotions have a lot to do with purring. Whether the false vocal cord theory, the muscle contraction theory, the turbulent blood theory, or some yet to be discovered theory turns out to be what makes Kitty purr, I think it's safe to say that at the root of it all we'll find the one thing that almost all cat owners already know and don't need scientists to tell them. Kitty is smart, Kitty is clever, and Kitty is certainly capable of feeling a wide range of emotions. Purring is just her way of letting us know about some of them.

KITTYSPEAK CONTINUED— OTHER VOCALIZATIONS
TALKATIVE CATS

Some cats are the strong, silent type like Sylvester Stallone, and others are like Joan Rivers—adorable, nonstop talkers. Some owners would give their right arm to have more talkative cats and others would give away their homes just to get their cats to shut up. You know how it is—the catnip is always greener on the other side of the fence.

Several elements help determine the degree to which Kitty naturally converses. Sometimes it's genetic, a simple case of breeding and ancestry, part of Kitty's inherent personality. Many Siamese cat owners will vouch for this. Other times it's actually a phenomenon taught by Mama Cat. A mother's talkative influence sometimes helps create talkative kids. Other Kitty conversationalists, believe it or not, are created by owners who have come to understand the finer points of animal language. Since breeding and what Kitty's mama might have done are out of your hands, there's not much you can do about them. However, if you really do want a more vocal cat pal you can learn the basic elements of Kittyspeak and encourage Kitty to talk more.

THE FINE ART OF KITTY CONVERSATION

By using verbal Kittyspeak, you can have legitimate down-home conversations with your cat. Practice your own meows and you'll find ones to which your Kitty responds. Once you connect with your cat through meows, you'll have to experiment as to the meanings of those sounds. It's easiest if you try to emulate her sound and tone when she's meowing for a particular purpose. Practice a little and she'll catch on—and so will you.

For cats who have been taught to make eye contact, as all of mine have, conversations are enhanced when that contact takes place. Kitty and you will be able to speak very succinctly to each other from opposite sides of the room. I guarantee that in almost every case, Kitty will so appreciate the conversation that in no time she'll bound over and into your lap for even more personal communication.

TRANSLATING THE MEOWS AND MEWS

The Kittyspeak vocabulary usually has a whole variety of meows. As a general rule, a lot of those meows mean very different things.

Meows can be loud and demanding, like when your cat wants to know in no uncertain terms whether, among other things, dinner is ready.

Meows can be short and sweet—more in the *mew* category. These usually come when Kitty is asking for something that she knows she has no right to expect, like some of your meal right after she's been fed. Mews are the tiniest little meows, often a holdover from kittenhood. I believe that Kitty developed these adorable mews just to melt our hearts and make us give in to whatever she wants. There's just no remaining hardhearted when that tiny, barely audible mew comes your way. Mowdy has mastered the mew. Of course, I'm convinced Mowdy attended classes at the School for the Performing Arts. Clark Gable and Sir Laurence Olivier could have learned a thing or two from my cat.

On the other end of the vocalization spectrum, meows can be *yowls*—most often indicating that Kitty's in pain, or something's wrong, or he's saying, "The heck with what you're doing, I want you to spend some time with me *now!*" Very intelligent cats will sometimes yowl to grab your attention when the more conventional meows have been ignored. Any way you look at it, there's no mistaking or ignoring Kitty's yowl. Although it doesn't have to be, a yowl could be a serious sign of distress. It pays to be a cautious owner. So make it a habit to double check that your cat is safe and sound whenever you hear a yowl.

- *The fighting screech*—Anyone who's been awakened at 3:00 A.M. by a cat fight taking place underneath the bedroom window knows how alarming this sound can be. Cat-fighting screeches are unmistakable—and that's Kitty's intent. Tough-sounding cats may never have to prove themselves in hand-to-hand—or paw-to-paw—combat. Act tough and the other kitty might just take off for home with his tail between his legs. If one cat doesn't retreat, the screeching often continues throughout the fighting. The sound seems to be an energizing feature for the cat much the same way a martial arts master might shout out as he strikes his blows.
- *Hissing*—There's usually no mistaking hissing and spitting. When you hear it, you know your cat means business and you'd better back off. Hissing is nature's way of letting other animals know that Kitty is ready and willing to deal with anyone that messes with her. I've heard some experts say that cats learned their hissing technique from mimicking snakes, the one animal most other animals respect. I'm not so sure I believe that Kitty does snake impressions. I have a feeling cats were capable of developing their own warning system without having to borrow it from any other animal.
- *A variety of in-between meows*—Uttered at different pitches with varying degrees of intensity, these can mean different things for different cats—hunger, contentedness, "let me out," "let me in," and so forth. If you listen closely you'll be able to differentiate between them. But, if you find that your ear for language isn't as good as what you'd hoped . . .

TAPE-RECORD KITTY

Really nutty cat owners, like me, get a kick out of tape-recording Kitty's sounds, making notes as to what was taking place at the time, and what he might have been saying. After accumulating a few recordings, it's fun and often enlightening to compare the meows. You'll learn that some meows recorded at different times, but under similar circumstances, are almost identical and that you were right on target as to what they meant. In other cases you'll learn how wrong you were when what you thought were similar meows are compared. When you find out your mistakes you'll be able to improve and adjust your language technique. It's a great home research project. When you stop to think of how many years you'll own Kitty, the tape-recording idea isn't as farfetched as it might sound. If the recording comparisons enhance even one point of communication, it's more than worth the effort.

- *Listen closely*—Cat owners with a normal interest in understanding Kitty may be content just to understand what she is saying. However, truly devoted, cat-crazy aficionados cannot stop there. We believe that when Kitty speaks, it's only fair that we sometimes talk back to her in her own language. You want her to understand English and increase her vocabulary, so continue conversing with her in *our* language. But if you want to take Kittyspeak to its fullest, try talking to Kitty in her *own* language. She'll appreciate your effort and you'll see the sparkle in her eyes when you connect. Fair is fair—Kitty should learn your language, but you need to make the attempt to learn hers, too.

TAPE-RECORD YOURSELF

If you really want to go all the way with Kittyspeak, try tape-recording yourself as you practice the varying degrees of meows and mews. At first you'll see there's plenty of room for improvement but I bet you'll pick up on it. Learning where improvement needs to be made is simple once you hear it on tape. In no time you'll hit your stride and Kitty will jump up right alongside you and the tape recorder. She'll know something's going on. As she makes her verbal inquiries, try responding in kind. Before you know it, you and Kitty will be engaged in a full-fledged conversation. Don't be embarrassed about mistakes in your grammar or pronunciation—Kitty will forgive you.

BODY LANGUAGE

As I said earlier, an important part of Kittyspeak is body language. It's no accident that Kitty holds her tail a certain way or tilts her head in an attempt to understand. She can look cute enough to turn your heart to mush or look so ferocious that even Arnold Schwarzenegger might think twice before picking her up.

Cats tell us a lot just by the way they carry themselves. Their physical demeanor communicates tremendous amounts of information. In order to better understand Kitty, it's important to learn this part of her vocabulary. Take Charlie Cat for example . . .

Charlie was owned by someone who didn't have a clue as to what he was saying. As a matter of fact, Charlie's owner didn't even realize her cat frequently tried to communicate through body language, a typical human assumption of superiority. But Charlie set the record straight.

Charlie's owner began seeing a new male companion and Charlie didn't like him—no way, no how. At first when the boyfriend came to the house, Charlie just stood his ground, glaring, tail bristling. After a few weeks, Charlie's behavior progressed—or deteriorated—depending on your point of view. He started giving the boyfriend a quick swat each time he walked by. Little sneak attacks. Then the big payoff came— Charlie piddled in the boyfriend's shoe. Unaware of this, the boyfriend placed his foot smartly and solidly into his Italian, supersoft leather loafer, complete with the piddle puddle. Charlie's owner thought it was pretty funny but the boyfriend was incensed. The more she laughed the more agitated he became. He started chasing Charlie all over the apartment, his dripping wet foot leaving moist footprints on the highly polished floor. He couldn't catch Charlie and his rage increased to the point where he grabbed an umbrella and took violent lunging swings every time Charlie was within striking distance. Escaping each time, Charlie's fleet feet made the boyfriend even crazier. When Charlie's owner sensed that things were getting out of hand, she jumped between the two of them to break it up. Containing his rage no further, the boyfriend knocked his girlfriend to the ground. In an instant Charlie sprang on top of him, his outstretched claws digging down the back of the man's head, then the side of his face and his neck. The boyfriend wrestled free from Charlie and ran from the apartment, one shoe on and one shoe off, leaving more wet footprints and blood droplets all the way down the hall to the elevator.

After the shock of the situation wore off, it began to settle into the mind of Charlie's owner that the cat was not to blame. Quite the opposite. Charlie had sensed that something was wrong with the boyfriend; he had picked up on things the owner was too blind to see. The boyfriend's true volatile personality was exposed for the first time when Charlie challenged him.

Charlie communicated his distrust and dislike through his body language. He had glared at the boyfriend for weeks, had started swatting at him, and then actually left a puddle in the man's shoe. Charlie was being very clear as to what he was saying and what he saw, but his owner wasn't taking the time to really listen to him. Had she paid attention to the way he was speaking to her, she would have realized something was wrong.

I place a lot of confidence in what animals tell me through their body language. If there are any nonbelievers among you, at least consider this: If you have a normally friendly, pleasant cat who enjoys everyone's company but takes a dislike to one particular person, *pay attention*. Cats have an uncanny way of picking up on the innuendos of personality, behavior, *and* body language. In the wild, they live or die by their assessments of other animals. The something extra that Kitty picks up on should not be casually disregarded. You'll often find that Kitty knows best.

HOW DID I KNOW KITTY HAD A TOOTHACHE?

If you know your cat and you've carefully observed his body language during healthy times, it's easy to observe when something's wrong. When you compare an unhealthy body language to Kitty's normal happy-go-lucky activities, you don't have to be a pet psychic to sense something is out of whack.

How your cat moves or doesn't move certain body parts can tell you how he is feeling or planning to react in the near future. Each cat is different, so the only rule of thumb is: Owners, know thine own cat and use the following explanations only as a guide.

THE EYES

Eyes tell me more about an animal I'm working with than any other factor. I believe the eyes *are* the mirror of the soul. Whether you're doing business over lunch and you need to assess the person sitting next to you, or whether you're dealing with ferocious lions, a gentle ape, or the cat in your home, close observation of the eyes will tell you more than a lot of other combined factors. When you're assessing a cat's general behavior, the eyes can be a dead giveaway as to what's coming next.

- *Wide-open eyes*—Obviously Kitty's awake, up and around, and alert. Observe the difference between normal wide-open eyes and wide-open eyes that have a mischievous glint. That glint is a dead giveaway that Kitty's up to no good. Be aware of that glint and you'll be able to stop that little whippersnapper before she gets into any trouble.

- *Half-closed eyes*—This means Kitty's relaxed, floating somewhere between being awake and napping. If Kitty happens to be on your lap at the time, sort of dozing off, he's showing you that he trusts you to a certain degree. If half-closed eyes occur at times other than when Kitty's nodding off, keep your own eyes open for signs of illness. If Kitty doesn't feel well his body language may be something less than bright-eyed and bushy-tailed.
- *Closed eyes*—Kitty's asleep or pretty close to it. If she'll allow herself to nod off in your presence, or again on your lap, that's the ultimate vote of confidence. She trusts you implicitly and knows you'd never hurt her.
- *Snoring with closed eyes*—What can I say? You lucky devil, Kitty's *totally* relaxed. Ear plugs, anyone?
- *Dilated and enlarged pupils vs. contracted pupil slits*—Both enlarged pupils and pupils that seem to close up into the smallest slits can be indicative of pending aggression. Sometimes the slit reflects a feeling of being threatened. The slit-eyed cat may be forced, by fear, into possible aggression. On the other hand, when a cat is the aggressor, actually instigating the situation, the pupils are usually enlarged or dilated. Either way, these looks should tip you off to a possible aggravated condition that could lead to aggression, complete with swatting, batting, or biting. Kitty's eyes are saying "handle with care," so until you know exactly what she means, take a safe approach.
- *Other circumstances for slit eyes*—To reduce the amount of light entering the eye so Kitty can see better, and for better perception of close objects.
- *Other circumstances for dilated pupils*—to increase the amount of light entering the eye so Kitty can see better.

THE MOUTH

Kitty's mouth speaks for itself: no pun intended. It's either relaxed in a comfortable position, uttering normal meows, or displaying some form of open-mouthed, raised-lip warning. Usually, the higher the raised or curled lip, the greater the degree of aggression being displayed. But don't count on that assessment alone. Any curled lip should be taken seriously.

For health reasons, watch for any excessive pawing or rubbing of the mouth and face areas. This is how you may be able to tell if Kitty does have that toothache, earache, or something in her eye.

THE WHISKERS

Happy little kitties keep their whiskers outwardly extended from the mouth area. If the whiskers are either pulled back tight along the face or are bristling, *watch out*—Kitty isn't happy. Aggression, or fear with the possibility of turning *into* aggression, is taking place. Pulled-back whiskers could also mean Kitty isn't feeling very well at all.

THE EARS

Ears can indicate a pet's mood and purpose, and, since they're quite easy to see, are good tools for interpreting body language quickly. Their little tiny pricked ears can tell us a lot. (A little kitty tidbit: The ears on Scottish Folds and American Curl Cats don't stand up in the normal manner and can't be counted on as easily when you interpret body language.)

- *Relaxed but normally alert ears* will move a little while changing direction as they pick up on sounds around them.
- *Submissive and fearful ears* are usually pulled back, lying flat against the head. They're in a perfect position to show another animal that Kitty would just as soon give in and let bygones be bygones, rather than getting involved in an aggressive entanglement. When attacked, cats may even pull

back their ears to lessen the chance of an ear being grabbed, bitten, or damaged. But don't be fooled by submissive ears. If feeling sufficiently challenged, any fearfully submissive animal is capable of shifting gears and attacking for its own self-preservation.

* *Full-blown aggressive ears* are usually out of their normal position but not quite flat against the head. They're often somewhat rotated so that a portion of the back of the ear is almost facing forward. This ear position says, "Hey, I'm ready for whatever comes my way and you're not scaring me off!"
* *Twitching ears* can occur with some cats at any emotional extreme, be it sheer delight, submission, or aggression.
* *Cats that aren't feeling well* may pull back their ears in various positions, depending on the degree of pain and physical upset. Usually, the more pulled back the ears, the greater the pain or upset.

THE TAIL

Cat owners are usually familiar with tails. Haven't we all awakened with one of them in our mouths at one time or another as Kitty snuggled close? Tails have a lot more to do with a cat's behavior than just being an inconvenient body part of a bedtime partner. In fact, I think tails are probably the most misunderstood body part of cats. I wish I had a dollar for every person who's been bitten or attacked by an animal he or she thought was friendly just because the tail was wagging.

* *Happy tails* can take on a few postures. One happy tail display is really no display at all: It is neither up nor down, not swooshing or moving, but just hanging there in a casual manner. This is Kitty's relaxed mode, when she's feeling pretty comfortable with the world around her.
  Another happy tail position is often greeted by owners with

bated breath. This happy little tail is held erect, directly over the tush, and is combined with a certain quivering motion. For any owner who has survived a spraying cat, it's reminiscent of the tail position for spraying and marking territory. It looks the same but this time, thank the cat gods, no spray is emitted. The same tail posture can be seen in cats that are happily excited about other things, particularly feeding time.

- *Aggressive tails* are crucial to recognize. It's important to understand that aggressive tails can also be fearful tails. Remember that the cat, if sufficiently frightened or threatened, might attack. Hence, aggressive and frightened tails can have the same body language.

  Tails that thump or swish from side to side are signs to look out for. Usually the faster and harder the tail swishes or thumps, the greater degree of the cat's aggression. Cats do not wag their tails in happy displays the way dogs do (although, never assume a dog's wagging tail indicates he's friendly). Misconstrue his tail position and you may walk away with a bloody badge of honor—but I guarantee you'll remember it the next time.

  Bristling tails held in an upright, arched, or curved position are other fairly obvious signs of the uncertain behavior that could be coming next. The key here is to watch for bristling fur.

- *Submissive tails*—As I mentioned before, it's often hard to tell the difference between a submissive posture and a potentially aggressive one. Submissive cats may also thump their tails as they move them back and forth. Other times a cat will lower his tail, literally between his legs, and run away in the most traditional sense of submissive body language. The most submissive, frightened cat may be found with his tail and entire body curled up in a ball, possibly whimpering and cringing.

- *Inquisitive tails*—Curious kitties display a tail that's raised up a bit but maintained in its normal, gently curved position.

• *Balancing tails*—Tails also act as a balancing agent, helping cats distribute their weight when they find themselves in precarious situations.
• *Sick cats* will often hold their tails in one of the submissive positions. Very often, the more submissive the tail position, the greater the illness or pain.

STRETCHING, YAWNING, AND ROLLING OVER ON THE BACK

Don't misinterpret comfy Kitty's stretching, yawning, and rolling over on her back, exposing her belly. Owners shouldn't run right over to join in what looks like an adorable play session and immediately try to rub the stomach. Depending on your relationship with Kitty, this could be greeted well or nervously, complete with a swat or bite. This position shows that Kitty is comfortable enough to be relaxed with you and is exposing the most vulnerable part of her body, the belly, but she may not be fully prepared for you touching her there.

BUMPING HEADS AND RUBBING NOSES

Kitty's most elaborate greeting may include a lot of head activity, such as bumping her head against you or rubbing her nose. Whether that's a way for her to distribute her scent or to make close personal contact with you, I think only the cats will ever know. In any event, take it as a compliment.

LICKING

If Kitty develops an obsession with licking a specific spot on her body, it's often her way of telling you there's pain in that area. Be sure you have the vet check it out. If Kitty's A-OK but continues licking, creating a lick granuloma (an extremely raw area), it could be a psychological problem, with its roots planted firmly in boredom or stress.

BE A GOOD CAT OBSERVER

Pay attention to Kitty's body language and you'll be pleased with the results. Not only will you better understand your furry little companion, but you may be able to pick up early warning signs indicating illness. Enlisting quick aid from a vet may save Kitty from some serious suffering—or worse. I'm sure you believe Kitty's worth that much, so attune your eyes and learn how to observe her. Kitty's giving you all the answers—all you have to do is look.

A GENTLE TOUCH

Think about how most cats are handled. How often do owners lift them up with one hand, grabbing them somewhere around the middle of their stomach? Poor Kitty dangles in the air and the stress from her body weight is placed directly in the middle of her belly. Would you like to be held like this while you dangled five or six feet above the ground? It certainly doesn't sound comfortable. As a matter of fact, I think it would hurt—a lot.

How many times have you dropped Kitty to the floor from a height of a foot or more? Cats are small creatures, often no larger than a newborn infant. Would you handle an infant like that?

When you touch Kitty, do it ever so gently. A soothing touch will convey a lot to our fragile furball. She'll come to trust the calm in your hands. She'll know you're sensitive, and she'll feel the concern and love you're transmitting.

HANDLE WITH CARE

If you've been carrying Kitty around, please place her down gently. Don't release your hold until she's on the floor and steady on her feet.

Please don't hold Kitty over your head—it looks like a long way down from her perspective. Instead, get down on the floor and spend more time at her level.

Whether you're educating Kitty and practicing her commands, or just cuddled up for a Sunday afternoon nap, handle your cat with care. Hold and stroke her in a special way. Soothe her when she's ill. Kitty will sense what you're doing and your gentle touch will let her know how much you love her. She'll love you for understanding.

MAKING DIRECT
EYE CONTACT—A MUST FOR A
HIGHLY DEVELOPED RELATIONSHIP

Here I go again. . . . I vehemently disagree with all the experts who say you shouldn't make direct eye contact with your pet, particularly sustained contact. While I certainly agree that direct eye contact may not be a good idea with animals who don't know you (they may view it as a threatening gesture), I see no reason to avoid eye contact with your pet pals. If anything, I believe that direct eye contact can add a new dimension to your relationship with your pet.

When Mowdy arrived on the scene, he was very adept at making eye contact as he peered in through my office window. His eyes would lock with mine and he'd scream at me to let him in. This was no shy little kitty. But the moment he was allowed in the house, he seemed unable to make direct eye contact with me. As tough and rough as he tried to be, Mowdy, like many other cats, is quite sensitive, a bit on the insecure side. I immediately went to work to bring him out of his reserved attitude. Now Mowdy marches—and I mean marches—into a room, looks me squarely in the eye, and in no uncertain terms tells me exactly what's on his mind.

WHY EYE CONTACT IS SO IMPORTANT

Cats are tiny little creatures living in a world that's so much larger than they are. Unless they're encouraged to make eye contact, they may never know that your eyes and face are five to six feet up in the air. As an experiment, lay flat on the floor and have someone stand over you. Strange feeling, isn't it?

This gives you an idea of what Kitty sees from her perspective. People who are friendly look something like the Jolly Green Giant; people who are upset, possibly correcting Kitty, look like tall, overwhelming ogres, scaring her like nothing she's ever known before. For a tiny kitty it's a mighty big world out there.

I don't think pet cats feel as threatened by direct eye contact as much as they feel uncomfortable. Most of their world revolves around things close to the ground—things that don't include human faces . . . unless you make your face more accessible to Kitty.

CRAWL AROUND ON THE FLOOR

Spend more time on the floor with Kitty. If you don't mind (come on, be a good sport), lie flat on your belly so that your face is really at her level. Don't feel silly. It's only right that you sometimes include yourself in Kitty's physical world. While you're there, encourage her to look at you. Talk to her sweetly and stroke her. Gently place your hands around the sides of her face and position it so she looks in your eyes. Continue to coo and talk to her sweetly. At first, Kitty may feel strange and pull away. Don't force her, just continue doing it a few times each day. In no time at all, Kitty will become more confident about facial contact and won't hesitate to look you squarely in the eyes. The ability to make direct eye contact will put you one foot (or paw) up on your relationship. As I said before, I believe the eyes mirror the soul. You'll be able to know so much more about Kitty and you'll be able to communicate on a level far superior to standard owner/cat relationships. Give it a shot. You'll be glad you did.

YOU DON'T HAVE TO BE
PSYCHIC TO UNDERSTAND YOUR CAT

Some people try to characterize what I do (understanding what a pet is saying) as the work of a pet psychic, blessed with special powers. I couldn't disagree more. I've simply learned to be a good observer. I prefer, rather, that I'm described as a modern-day Dr. Doolittle. Although I'm not sure I'm deserving of this flattery, it's the idea of talking to the animals as Dr. Doolittle once did that I most appreciate.

I believe that most of the people who say they have special powers as pet psychics have simply mastered the art of observation. I don't believe that mysterious brain wave messages are sent from Kitty's head to that of the psychic. But I do believe that the person can often interpret the signals of Kitty's body language and understand what Kitty is saying. Everyone possesses the same basic potential for using the power of observation. We all have a certain part of our brain that is underused. Our raw potential is there; we just don't do enough with it.

Psychic abilities over and above what I have described may exist. I fully believe there are greater powers than what science can support—it's just that I haven't yet seen any as they apply to pets. I've been in the same room with some of the most well-known pet psychics and I've yet to be impressed. In many cases I was actually embarrassed by their incorrect assessments or claims that the correct ones were due to psychic ability. In fact, being in the same room at the same time with the same animal and being provided with the same background on each animal, I could better their percentage of correct information simply by observing the animal's various behaviors and taking some educated guesses. You don't have to be a genius or blessed with special mental gifts to understand that a stray cat, having lived out a good part of his life on the streets, might be timid around strangers. Also, a cat with that background might be overly possessive of the person who took him in and showed him love and affection. That street Kitty may have an insatiable appetite as well, now that he has a chance to eat real food rather than meals from garbage pails. There's also a good possibility that he might hate other cats, since he could have had to fend them off while eking out an existence on the streets. Not too tough to figure out, huh?

Pet psychics? Give yourself more credit than that. As a loving owner you can learn to understand what your little bundle of fur is saying, feeling, and thinking. Open your eyes and ears. Take a good hard look, and keep at it during Kitty's life. Don't quit after the novelty of the adorable, fuzzy kitten wears off. Talking to your four-footed pal should be an ongoing dialogue; the more you fine tune the skills, the more information you'll be able to send back and forth. Just you and little Kitty. Leave the crystal ball for somebody else.

3

❧   ❧   ❧

WHY DOES KITTY
DO THAT?

WHY KITTY CHASES
AND GRABS YOU

Ever wonder what's behind Kitty's attempt to pounce and wrap herself around your ankle? Think about it from her point of view. There are these moving objects (your feet) quickly running down the hallway. An alarm goes off in her head. "Hey, this looks like fun. Let's go chase them." She does—and in seconds your ankles are caught and held hostage.

Sometimes this action is accompanied by a little nip or a few claws placed strategically around your ankle bone. And, yes, sometimes it hurts. This may not be much of a consolation to your battered, bruised or bloodied ankles, but Kitty's action is just a flashback to generations ago when chasing after a moving target meant there would be dinner that night. It's also just a good way to pass some time on a lazy afternoon.

If Kitty should make you or other people the target of her commando tactics, try to nicely dissuade her. Tell her no and be consistent about it—but whatever you do don't be harsh or overly corrective. Understand that Kitty's instincts are surfacing and by coming down too hard on her you may create one neurotic Kitty. Instead, gradually ease the furry Rambo out of her feet-hunting ways by concentrating on those things that she is allowed to chase. Experiment with different toys and games until you find the ones that bring out this side of her behavior.

Let her release chase energy at appropriate times and you'll find that she'll slowly decrease her pouncing on your ankles.

Some people will certainly disagree with me. They're sure to say that by encouraging Kitty to chase after "allowed" items I'm simply stimulating the stalking part of her behavior. However, I believe that the chase is normal behavior for cats. Asking Kitty not to participate in it is like telling little kids not to run. With kids you teach them that zooming around in the house is forbidden but playing outside is okay. It's no different with little Kitty. It's simply a matter of fine-tuning what can and cannot be pounced on.

Your ankles will be safe once again.

WHY KITTY RUBS UP AGAINST YOU

Here's another Warren Eckstein opinion that differs from that of a lot of other experts.

Many experts think that cats rub up against people and things in order to transfer their scent. By rubbing up against something, cats smear their odor all over, claiming it as a part of their territory.

While I don't dispute this, I believe that Kitty rubs against things for another reason, too. I simply can't buy into the suggestion that, after living in the same house with the same family for years, a cat needs to leave her scent all over the people and things already reeking of her Kitty odor. I believe that Kitty also rubs when she's excited. A wound-up Kitty can't sit at a desk and tap her fingernails on it. She can't reach for a cigarette or a pack of gum. She's excited and feels a need to move and do things, but her options are limited. So she rubs.

And let's not overlook the obvious either. Sometimes you just have to scratch your back. Four tiny little paws, no matter how they stretch and strain, can't always reach the spot. Rubbing up against something can certainly do the trick.

WHY KITTY KNEADS

When Kitty's relaxing on your lap or on a soft blanket, do you ever wonder why he lifts one paw, then presses it back down, over and over again, repeating this rhythmic process while he seems to be in another world? This is called kneading, or trampling. When Kitty is content he reverts back to his kittenhood—when kneading on his mom's belly was an important part of nursing. (Kneading actually helps Mama Kitty produce milk at the right time.)

The next time your little furball kneads on your lap and his nails stick into you like daggers, try not to yell and jump up with a start. Poor little Kitty won't understand, and you'll only confuse him. He's simply shifting back to a time in his life when Mama was important. I know it's hard, but try to take it as a positive response.

TELEPHONE KITTY

Ever wonder why Kitty gets so demanding when you're on the phone? If you own a cat who won't give you any peace—jumping up to see you and saying hello—while you're talking on the telephone, think about this for a moment:

You're talking. Kitty doesn't see anyone else around. She comes in, jumps up, rubs around you, and in general, makes a royal nuisance out of herself. It gets to the point where you think she's jealous or spiteful because you're spending time doing something other than loving and playing with her.

Well, that's simply not true! As far as Kitty is concerned you are talking to *her!* After all, no one else is around—so who else could you be talking to? Cats are clever but no one has yet been able to explain to them the miracles of modern technology. So the next time telephone Kitty comes around and bothers you, don't scold her, that's not fair. Your cat legitimately thinks that your voice is meant for her ears.

4

❀ ❀ ❀

KITTY'S MENTAL HEALTH

RECOGNIZING YOUR CAT'S EMOTIONS

It wasn't so long ago that some of the press had plenty of fun at my expense. In the early 1970s various newspaper and magazine articles referred to me as the world's first pet psychologist—a feline Freud and puppy shrink. Reporters giggled, envisioning a pet lying on the couch, with me sitting alongside listening intently and taking notes. Some drew cartoon caricatures. Others even went to the trouble of setting up elaborate photographs, with one caption reading "America's first psychologist for pets."

I've never been one to take offense at someone poking fun at what I do. If you're not having a good time when it comes to pets and animals, then you're in the wrong business. However, I can say that I have taken great pleasure in having the last laugh. What was virtually unheard of in the early 1970s is now widely accepted. I'm extremely proud that in the early days I was right out there, in the trenches pouring out my message to anyone who would listen.

Cats are living, feeling creatures. They laugh. They frown. They can feel lonely and depressed, as well as upset and stressed. Simply stated, I believe pets are fully capable of experiencing the same—or a very similar—range of emotions as their human counterparts. They may not experience it in exactly the same way, but they do experience it nonetheless.

Well, I'm certainly no Sigmund Freud and I don't believe that a cat owner has to be an expert in psychology in order to recognize Kitty's various emotional states. But problems surface when owners don't believe that Kitty has mental health needs. Trouble also arises when owners do recognize Kitty's emotional range but don't know what that range includes, what precisely to look for, and what to do if there is an emotional disturbance.

That's why I wanted to devote an entire section to Kitty's psyche. Her psyche can be as delicate as she is but it can also be surprisingly tough. A little bit of knowledge can help you recognize Kitty's ups and downs, her highs and lows. Best of all, the knowledge will help you detect early warning signs, allowing you to intervene before Kitty gets in too deep, ensuring her mental well-being. Mental health is just as important to Kitty as her physical health.

Welcome to the world of modern day pet behavior analysis.

KITTY STRESS

Life in industrialized nations has taken its toll on people and animals. Certainly Kitty has felt the demands. She now spends more time alone because the family is working or busy. Owners come home tired and burned-out from being on the job and Kitty senses that, too. It's easy for her to pick up on the body language of her owners and in turn she feels and reacts to the owners' tension and stress. Can Kitty feel the pressure? The answer is a loud and resounding yes!

Moving, illness, boarding stays, and even marital problems can also affect the little furball. So the next time you're ready to argue in front of your cat, think about it. Does Kitty really need the extra stress in her life? She sure doesn't—and you probably don't either. Take a deep breath and forget about it—at least for Kitty's sake!

MENTAL STIMULATION FOR
GOOD MENTAL HEALTH

I bet you've never given your cat's mental health much thought. Well, throughout this book you'll find many references to the fact that cats are intelligent, curious, and emotional creatures. You'll also find me on a perpetual bandwagon espousing the need for owners to pay more attention to keeping Kitty's mind active. Since virtually no one else is talking about this crucial area of cat care, I feel I need to keep driving home the point. Inactive minds can lead us down the garden path to a lot of unwanted bad behavior habits and can create unhealthy mental attitudes that do nothing but detract from Kitty's physical well-being. I firmly believe that the body works as a unit. That means both physical and mental health play equal supporting roles to make up the whole.

More and more studies are demonstrating that psychological stress can weaken a human's ability to fight off illness and disease. I'm thoroughly convinced the same holds true for little Kitty. I'm also convinced that most cat owners do not pay nearly enough attention to their beloved pets' frame of mind. It's not that they're cruel or abusive, it's just that no one ever points out Kitty's needs for good mental health. When you take a hard look at things, it's clear that many of today's cats are kept indoors all or most of the time, living in homes where everyone works or is out of the house all day. What a life— sleeping late into the morning, then taking an even later morning nap, then napping in the early afternoon and again in the late afternoon. In between snoozing, there's a little aimless wandering around the house. Although I'd certainly like to do that for a few weeks, I know it would get old and tedious quickly. It's boring, routine and oh so humdrum.

That's pretty much what happened with some former clients of mine, two of David Letterman's pets, Bob and Stan. Dave had a grueling schedule with his new television show, so Bob and Stan spent a lot of time alone. Also, the adjustment from a freewheeling life in Malibu, California, to a confined New York City apartment helped aggravate some aggressive behavioral problems. Urban life just didn't hold a candle to their old beachfront playground and that had a negative effect on their psychological well-being.

DON'T MISS THE CHANCE TO DO ONE OF THE MOST IMPORTANT THINGS YOU CAN FOR YOUR CAT

You'll find that I've included several chapters in this book that deal specifically with psychological problems. I've also included dozens of suggestions about things you can do to keep Kitty on her toes, properly stimulated, and less stressed—all of which will help keep her both physically and mentally healthy and sharp.

Concentrate on good mental health through the use of mental stimulation. Don't be lulled into thinking that everything's okay with your cat. Think about a party or a picnic for Kitty. Spice up her life. You'll probaby be surprised by the changes you see. Most of my clients don't realize their cats need anything more than normal affection, but once they get started on my program, they notice a lot of subtle changes in Kitty's behavior and appearance: a healthy glow and increased enthusiasm and vigor. When all those small improvements come together and combine into the larger whole, the cat turns into a very different kitty, one that's certainly better off for your effort.

CAT DEPRESSION—IS IT REAL
OR ARE WE CRAZY?

Can cats become depressed? Will Kitty need to cuddle up next to his own personal Valium bottle? Does she need a pet shrink to straighten out her head?

Controversy rages over whether cats have the emotional capacity to become depressed, provoking heated responses from people with opinions on both sides of the question. Believers in cat depression say, "Of course they become depressed. It's obvious by their behavior and it makes common sense." But non-believers argue that the thought of cats having the emotional capacity for depression is anthropomorphic. They say cat-loving animal fanatics attribute human behavior to their pets and it is the owners, not their cats, who are emotionally unstable by thinking of animals in human terms. Both sides argue their points with great conviction.

Actually, the disagreement centers on new behavioral theories, pets' emotional capabilities, and how they interact within families. With new ideas there are always bound to be skeptics. I believe anyone who has had a close relationship with a cat knows unequivocally that a cat can become depressed. Cats have a wide range of emotions and depression is certainly possible. Also, anyone taking the opposite point of view may be spending too much time in the laboratory, officially testing these sorts of things, and not nearly enough time building a special relationship with a cat.

I've seen many pets mourn their deceased masters or special play pals, and I've seen them turn lethargic, wandering all over the house looking for junior after he's moved out to go to college. Divorce also plays a big part in creating depressed cats. They don't understand the arguments and general upheaval that normally accompany a divorce. They certainly don't understand when, all of a sudden, family members and maybe even the kids disappear.

Depression brought about by mourning or a feeling of abandonment is very upsetting to Kitty, and her little eyes express the pain. It breaks your heart because she's so terribly confused—you wish you could explain it to her so she'd understand. Fortunately, extra tender loving care helps most pets out of this type of temporary depression. The pitfall here is that very often the owner is suffering through similar personal problems relating to a family member's death, divorce, or, after the kids move out, the empty nest syndrome. Busy coping with their own problems, owners sometimes forget that Kitty needs a different, caring type of attention during the same period of time. She needs to be soothed when there's so much emotional upheaval and she desperately needs compassion. Owners, please be aware of your cat's needs during these difficult times. I know it's hard to think of your cat when your life has just been torn apart, but sharing your grief with Kitty will certainly help her. It will more than likely help you, too. A snuggling little Kitty makes us all feel better.

Divorce, the death of a friend or family member, or the kids going off to college are obvious causes of depression and because of the abrupt change in Kitty's life they're often easy to recognize. But can you recognize the type of depression that may be killing off your cat a little at a time? Consider this scenario:

You've been fairly busy for more days or weeks than you care to remember. There just isn't enough time in the day. The cat gets underfoot, yowling for food for the fourth time that day, and you've got a million things to do. You yell. Kitty pulls back her ears and slinks off to the corner. Placing her head down, she watches every move you make with big bulging eyes. She's hoping against hope that maybe you'll have a little time for her. But you don't. There's too much work to be done, too many errands to run. You promise yourself that you'll find some time tomorrow to play with her and give her plenty of special attention. Tomorrow comes and you're still busy. The cat finds herself treated as if she's part of the furniture. The next day it's still the same. But the following day, wow! You play, and even split a little specially cooked chicken with her. Then the next three weeks come and go and you're very busy again. Haven't you noticed by now that sweet Kitty is withering away?

Neglect is the #1 cause of depression in our cats. It happens so gradually most of us don't see it coming, then "all of a sudden" the cat looks old. It sneaks up slowly until one day you realize what you've done and the effect it's had on your cat.

That's what happened to Millie. At three years old she was a very adorable orange-tan cat with the cutest white spots on her face and big white spots on three of her four paws. It looked as if she were wearing socks, except that she forgot to put one of them on. Millie was owned by a fairly successful young couple who was on the business track to bigger and better things. In order to climb their respective corporate ladders they worked excruciatingly long, hard hours. They wanted a pet to enjoy, but because of their long work week they didn't think it would be fair to own a dog. Deciding to be good Samaritans, they went to the local animal shelter and adopted Millie just before she was going to be put to sleep.

Her allotted time at the shelter was almost up, with no potential adopters in sight. Millie lucked out in that respect. She was plucked from the shelter only hours before she was slated to be killed.

In the beginning, everything was terrific—plenty of attention, love, and affection. Millie thrived. She was perky and playful and very adorable. The owners even left the office a little earlier or stopped home on lunch breaks to make sure Millie was okay. Since it was a new environment they didn't want her to get too lonely.

Because everything was so perfect it was easy for Millie's

owners to get lulled back to their old work habits—long hours
and business files to review when they arrived home. Their
dinners usually consisted of Chinese takeout. Who had time to
do the shopping, let alone cook? Sometimes even Millie's food
ran low, so out of convenience and sheer exhaustion the owners would create makeshift cat meals of human tuna, even
chicken chow mein. It reached the point where Millie wasn't
happy even with these special meals because she didn't like to
eat alone. It seemed that, for her, mealtime was in the kitchen
while everyone else ate in bed watching TV. Starved for affection, Millie opted to stay in the bedroom with her owners
and left her food in the kitchen. Food was taking a backseat to
attention and lots of leftover cat meals were thrown into the
garbage.

Millie seemed bored and started sleeping more. Since it was
wintertime, no one thought twice about it. Everyone seems less
active during winter, the owners rationalized. When spring
came it would be different. Millie developed a little cough at
night, but since her owners had more than a few allergies of
their own they didn't attribute the cough to anything special.
Most of the time they were so dog-tired at night, sleeping like
logs, they didn't hear Millie anyway. Millie's coat was getting
dull and dry but it was winter, and you know how drying
indoor heat can be, the owners thought. She looked a little thin
around the ribs but they convinced themselves that because her
coat was so dry it wasn't really her weight that was the
problem—it was just an illusion of a less dense coat. However,
they decided they'd take her to the vet anyway. They set up an
appointment but had to cancel it because of a late business
dinner. They promised the receptionist they'd set it up again
soon, but they didn't get around to it.

One day when they came home, Millie wasn't at the door to
greet them. She was lying on the bed barely able to move.
They rushed her over to the vet but it was way too late. Lovely

little Millie, with the funny little white spots on her face and three little white socks on her paws, didn't last out the night. Worst of all, she died in pain. Wonderful, sweet Millie, what did they do to you?

Did depression kill Millie? No, not quite. However, it is a case of what comes first, the chicken or the egg? The point is that when there is any problem with Kitty's mental health, particularly depression, many things start to factor in—diet and exercise are certainly two of them. As Kitty becomes a poor eater and spends less time exercising in the fresh air, her immune system gets progressively weaker. When the immune system weakens, Kitty is a prime candidate for almost any bacteria or viral infection that comes her way.

SIGNS OF DEPRESSION—WHAT TO LOOK FOR

The best way to know when something's wrong is to pay close attention to the cat's behavior when everything's right.

1. Take note of how much Kitty normally plays so you'll know when she develops an unenthusiastic attitude toward toys and games that once amused her.
2. How's her normal appetite? Has she always been finicky or moderately picky, or does she eat with gusto? Depressed cats often go off their feed. This is a particularly good clue when assessing depression, particularly when the vet gives Kitty a clean bill of health. A depressed appetite is often a red flag alerting owners to a depressed mental attitude.
3. Note the cat's sleeping habits. Nine times out of ten there will be signs of general inactivity. Cats suffering from depression tend to lounge around the house and do much less than cats who are in a good frame of mind.
4. Watch for lackluster effort in personal grooming habits. Most cats are fastidiously clean, licking and grooming themselves in an almost ritualistic manner. Depressed cats, like people, may not care about their own personal hygiene.

Owners may notice a sticky, dirty coat or more cat hair than usual on the carpet or furniture.

5. Be on the lookout for changes in behavior. Is the normally sweet kitty more aggressive, or is the normally very friendly, sociable cat hiding under the bed every time visitors come by? Any real change in behavior can be a sign of a much deeper problem.

6. Take a good look at your cat's eyes. Do they still reflect life's excitement, or is the sparkle gone? The eyes will let you know what your cat is feeling.

TRICKS FOR LIFTING YOUR CAT FROM THE DEPTHS OF DEPRESSION

Recognizing that your cat is depressed is the important first step. Knowing how to lift the cat from that depressed stage comes next. If you've been able to assess the damage and determine what might have triggered the problem, you're ahead of the game. You may be able to find a replacement for the loss of whatever caused Kitty to become depressed. If Kitty suffered the death of her companion cat, for example, you may find that adding a little kitty whippersnapper to the household is the solution. Or if you can't commit to another full-time pet, why not throw a few parties for your cat and invite some of her cat friends over for a change? "She doesn't have any friends," you say. Then boo on you! Cats need to have a few friends of their own. It's time to expand the cat's social calendar and develop a new circle of kitty comrades. Just be sure your cat and all invited guests get along well with other animals. And if your cat was used to a lot of household activity—complete with teenagers and plenty of foot traffic in and out—and now things are quiet, it may be time to repay some of those invitations that you owe. Throw a few dinner parties and lunches, this time for humans, in order to create more cat/human interaction.

It's not always easy to figure out what causes Kitty's low spirits. Often a really depressed state comes about from a combination of factors, not just one isolated reason. In such cases my preferred plan of attack is a well-varied program for perking up Kitty's life.

CHANGING THAT HO-HUM ROUTINE

The best way to put zip into a lackluster daily existence is to make some changes. Mix things up a little. Cats who don't quite know what to expect will begin to look forward to the uncertainties of the next day. Add some new flavors into the standard diet or cook something special once or twice a week. Buy lots of new toys and put most of the old ones away for another day. Try a little kitty massage (see page 153) or a kitty makeover (see page 190). Buy a catnip plant and let it grow, giving Kitty access to it from time to time. If she hasn't yet been taught to walk on a leash (see page 121), it's time to start. Get her out of the house. The same four walls can start to close in on any of us after a while. Take her to visit Grandma or the nieces and nephews. Odds are she'll love her special excursions and come home happy and content afterward.

Treat Kitty's depression like the serious, real problem it is, because an emotional valley, if left unchecked, can be as threatening to a cat's health and happiness as many other "real" medical problems. Don't laugh it off! If you believe your cat is depressed, don't be embarrassed by friends or relatives who think *you're* the one who's got the problem. As I've said before, cats are intelligent, sensitive animals and are just as capable as humans of experiencing a wide range of emotions. It's up to you to support the emotional needs of your precious little four-footed friend.

A QUICK TIP—THE BEST WAY TO RECOGNIZE DEPRESSION IN YOUR CAT

Find a picture of your cat from a year ago and compare it to how he looks today. Sure, he looks older, but is there something else? Take a good look at the eyes. Are they as happy to be alive as they were in the photo? If not, don't wait. Do something special together—now.

LATCHKEY KITTIES LEFT ALONE ALL DAY

You're probably asking yourself, "Just what *is* a latchkey cat?" Latchkey kitties, like latchkey kids, are left alone while adults are at work or out of the house, busy with errands and chores. The phrase latchkey kid was coined when women with children started joining the work force in droves. Their kids would come home from school, open the latches or locks with their personal set of keys, and walk into an empty house alone and on their own.

Latchkey cat is a phrase I coined not long after. Although Kitty's not actually struggling with a set of keys scrunched between her paws trying to let herself in, the concept is basically the same. With the increase of the two-income household with or without kids, the single head of a household, or just the plain old single household, mothers just aren't around the way they used to be when I was growing up. Even if Mom doesn't work she's usually running around during the day taking care of dozens of family errands.

In any type of household these days, Kitty is usually left alone most of the time.

What does being a latchkey pet mean to your cat? It means being alone probably eight to ten hours a day while you work; being alone another hour or two while you shop or go out for dinner, and alone again another eight hours while you're asleep. Add it up and what do you get? You get a cat that's left unattended anywhere from between sixteen to twenty hours out of every twenty-four-hour day. That's a lot of solitary time.

ARE WE ASKING TOO MUCH—
SHOULD A CAT BE A LATCHKEY CAT?

That's the next logical question. If you belong to a working or busy family, or if you live a busy single life-style, is it fair to own a cat? Yes, as long as you keep one very important point in mind. Quality time is more important than quantity time. Just because it's a cat doesn't mean it requires less attention than a dog. There should be no double standards when meeting the needs of pets.

FEELING GUILTY ABOUT LEAVING
THE FURBALL ALONE?
OR
THINKING ABOUT FINDING A NEW
HOME FOR KITTY?

Don't give up your little pal! There are no guarantees that the next home will be a loving home. Sometimes spending minutes with someone you love is more important than spending hours with someone you don't.

WHAT YOU CAN DO TO BE FAIR TO
YOUR LATCHKEY KITTY

Find a few special moments each day to spend with Kitty. Don't be a weekend parent and overdo things on Saturday and Sunday to make up for lost weekday time.

So that Kitty has something to do while you're out, take some of her favorite treats and hide them where she won't find them too easily, but will be able to locate eventually. As she wanders aimlessly around the house during the day she'll come across a little surprise here and there. It will help perk up her day and might even take her mind off that day's decision of whether to scratch up the new couch or leave little presents all over the expensive rug.

If the thought of leaving small food treats lying around brings nightmares of creepy crawly bugs coming into your home, consider buying an automatic feeder. It has a timer that can be set to uncover food dishes at appointed hours so Kitty always has a little nosh to break up the day. Check around—modern technology has improved upon the feeders of the past. I prefer the battery operated ones so that Kitty doesn't have electrical cords close to where she's chewing. Some newer versions can be set to open several times during the day and close gently so Kitty can't be hurt. The noise that accompanies the opening of the cover is enough to let her know it's snack time. If her food tends to spoil, seek out an automatic feeder that comes complete with ice packs that can be placed under the food dish area to keep things properly chilled. Kitty can then have her own little party even when no one's home. Now, what more could you ask for?

When you do come home, spend the first ten minutes with your cat. She'll be excited and all charged up to have someone around. If you don't give her some positive attention then, you'll be dealing with her stored-up, misguided energy all night long. If Kitty's really craving attention, she may even work her way into a negative attention syndrome. The little darling knows she's going to be yelled at but opts for negative, corrective attention rather than no attention at all. As I said before, these Kitty kids aren't much different than the human kids. So, in those first ten minutes when you walk in the door, play a little game she enjoys, then give her a few minutes of loving and hugging. She'll be better behaved all evening long and it will actually take you less time than if you have to constantly interrupt what you're doing to chase after and scold her as she desperately tries to get a reaction out of you.

At least two or three times a week, preferably more if you can, get Kitty out of the house. You know how I feel by now. Bring her to see Grandma or the kids. How about a special outing? Or being spectators at the local Little League game? Bring her to see a few kitty play pals. *Anything!* Just do *some-*

thing. I promise you, Kitty's not that fussy. She'll be grateful for any time away from the house. It will break up her monotonous routine and will stop those four walls from closing in. If you work in a small office, it might be possible to take Kitty to the job once in a while (just bring a portable litter box). If not, find ways to work her into your schedule. It won't take you any more time to bring Kitty along on a quick trip to the drive-in store. And since it's a drive-in, you won't have to leave Kitty unattended in the car.

Experiment with calling the little furball on the phone and leaving a message on the answering machine. Some cats love to hear your voice and know Mommy or Daddy is talking to them, while others are frustrated if they hear you but can't find you. Mowdy loves it. I call and let him know that Daddy will be home soon and we're going to play chase, his favorite game. (We chase each other around the living room table.) The only problem is that Mowdy always wins. But I can deal with that. After all, I've convinced myself he has the advantage. He has four legs.

If the answering machine doesn't work for you, try leaving a radio on that is set to a talk station. The voices may help Kitty get through the day.

Some cats like to hear a recorded family conversation that has been taped on a continuous-play cassette. With one, your kitty can have the comfort of the family's voices around her all day long. But here, too, as with the answering machine, you'll have to experiment to see if it helps or makes her frustrated when she can't find you in the house.

Get up ten minutes early in the morning and provide Kitty with some special playtime. If we expect Kitty to be good all day long, the least we can do is set the alarm clock a tad earlier than normal. Yes, I know it's hard to get up any earlier than necessary. If anything, it's a whole lot easier to push the snooze button and talk yourself into five more minutes of sleep. At those times, keep one thing in mind: If you really can't find an extra ten minutes to spend with Kitty before leaving for work, you might have to consider whether you have the time or proper attitude to own a cat in the first place.

Say good-bye when you leave the house. Have a little Kitty conversation. Some people say you should just leave and not make a big production out of it, but I couldn't disagree more. I think it's very important to give Mowdy a special good-bye in the morning. We have a private little hug and smooch, then I tell him I'll be back later and that he should be a good boy. He's come to know the routine and I know he finds the good-bye and personal contact very reassuring.

Say hello when you come home. Mowdy greets me at the door the instant I arrive home. It's the cutest thing to see Mowdy and his dog brother, Tige, sitting alongside each other just waiting to say hi. Tige is the dog from the Buster Brown commercials—you know, Buster Brown and his dog, Tige. Well, Tige doesn't live in a shoe, he lives with Mowdy and me. Together they act like my personal welcoming committee. So when your exclusive little fan club runs to the door to greet you, put down your packages and dry cleaning and give your four-legged friends the type of greeting they're giving you. It takes thirty seconds and I guarantee it means a lot to them.

Think about a pet pal for Kitty. A cat or dog friend may just be what he needs to pass the time (see page 75 for information on how to introduce a new pet into the house).

Latchkey cats are a special breed. At no other time in the history of man have pets been asked to stay cooped up and alone for so much of their lives. We're asking a lot of our cats to have to put up with this modern life-style. The least we can do is try to meet them halfway. It's only fair. It's only reasonable. It's the only humane thing to do.

KITTY'S MIDLIFE CRISIS

Please try to contain your laughter or disdain until you hear me out on this one. There comes a point in some cat owners' lives when the thrill is gone and the novelty of having a cat in the house has slowly worn thin. After all it took for Kitty and owner to settle in with each other, you'd think they could just sit back and enjoy the meeting of the minds for years to come. You know the sort of image I'm talking about—Mom's rocking back and forth in her favorite porch chair with a snuggly, middle-aged, happy cat on her lap. Well, I hate to break the bad news to you but it's not always so. The important words here are "middle-aged" and "happy." These words don't always go together. Often what happens is that the cat gets taken for granted. It's kind of like a comfortable old pair of slippers that fit perfectly—why bother looking for anything else even though they're worn, dirty, and need a change?

People suffer midlife crises all the time. They've spent a lot of years doing things they're not so certain were right for them. Sometimes a midlife crisis means a few minor adjustments—a different hair color, a new wardrobe, a change of job. Other times it means a lot more than that and there's a change of spouse or relocation to a new city. In any event, midlife often means a need for a change, a change to reinvigorate the mind and the body.

Can Kitty have a midlife crisis? You bet he can—particularly if his life has become one big routine, lacking in things that keep him interested and alert. He can become bored, depressed, less active, or experience a personality shift or almost any psychological or physical change you might also expect from a human being going through midlife difficulties.

So now that you're done laughing and understand that even Kitty can find himself in a midlife rut, just what should you do?

Well, Kitty can't dye her hair or go on a shopping spree. The best approach is preventive—never let it happen in the first place. You won't let it happen if you apply all the information in this book and keep Kitty mentally and physically stimulated throughout her years. Don't let her take a backseat to what goes on in your life. Cats who get pushed aside because of owners' busy life-styles are in the greatest jeopardy. However, cats owned by people who have fallen into their own monotonous daily routines are equally at risk. It's possible for an owner to be home with Kitty all day long and still not provide the type and quality of attention that's required.

If you suspect a midlife problem is affecting your cat, the resolution is fairly simple: Change things around. Make everything a little different—different food, excursions to parts unknown. Create a few surprises for the furball. Purchase a new litter box. Go shopping for a new Kitty wardrobe—a new leash, collar, or harness. Let her try on a couple of new sweaters. Take her on a picnic! And, please throw out that old disgusting scratching post and buy her two new ones. Buy her a big bunch of new toys! Develop a kitty toy chest, even if you think she won't play with toys anymore. You may be surprised by her interest in the new playthings. At the very least, she'll appreciate your effort. Go out of your way. A little extra TLC will keep Kitty emotionally happy and may even help her live a physically healthier life. Active happy cats don't get sick as often as listless cats. Pay attention to Kitty's state of mind—it will serve you well. It will do a lot for her, too.

Owners of young kittens, remember this chapter a few years from now. Owners of middle-aged cats, it's time to get a move on. What you do today can make a big difference in Kitty's vitality for years to come.

DO CATS CRY
EMOTIONAL TEARS?

This is a hot topic. Although there are many claims in support of this theory, scientists are skeptical about animals crying emotional tears. Hard evidence doesn't really exist, but there's so much anecdotal evidence that it's difficult to disregard it all.

It may be that not all animals cry emotional tears but it seems there's a likelihood that some do. Dian Fossey, the late gorilla expert, related a story about seeing Coco, one of her prized gorillas, cry for emotional reasons. Of the many gorillas Fossey worked with over the years, Coco's was the only such case, but this well-respected animal expert swore it was true.

Even Charles Darwin wrote an account of elephants shedding emotional tears. However, when questioned, many zookeepers and similar experts emphatically state that they have never seen an animal cry for emotional reasons. Their eyes may have watered and shed tears, they say, due to various physical elements, but not because of an emotional upset. Now that you've read the preceding sentence I would like you to consider a quote I read the other day from the director of one of the world's most famous zoos. It relates to a case of alleged animal abuse in his facility. I was astonished to read that he felt that the alleged abuse was unfounded—he felt that tying down an animal while several trainers and handlers beat it about its head and body was an appropriate method of dealing with an unwilling animal. The account concluded with him stating something to the effect that it was, after all, *just* an animal.

Well, if this is the type of mentality that is responding to the question of whether animals shed emotional tears, no wonder the answer is negative. I suspect this type of person wouldn't know an emotional tear if it slapped him in the face.

Can animals cry? Not too long ago I received a letter from a child who said that whenever she cried, her cat Muffy would cry with her. The little girl's parents ignored the story until one day after she had been punished the parents walked into her room and found two wet pillows and two wet faces.

I've opened up this question for discussion on several radio shows, and much to even *my* surprise amazing numbers of pet owners have come forth saying they have had similar experiences. Most of these seem to involve the loss of a family member or another family pet.

Although I've owned many cats in my day, I've never seen tears in any of them. However, the longer I own Mowdy, the more sensitive he becomes—and I definitely feel he has the potential to cry. The once rough-and-tumble tomcat, terror of the neighborhood, has slowly turned into a loving, emotional buddy. The local bully has changed. When he's upset it's very apparent. His eyes give him away.

FIRST KITTY PSYCHOLOGY— HOW TO INTRODUCE A SECOND PET TO YOUR CAT— AVOIDING FIGHTS

The third most frequently asked question popping up in my monthly mailbag of a thousand-plus letters is what to do about fighting between pets who live under the same roof. Anyone who guessed that pets leaving little accidents and presents all over the floor is the #1 problem is correct. So is a guess that the second most frequently asked question has to do with pets redecorating and redesigning the furniture by scratching and chewing. But how many people would suspect that the #3 problem on cat owners' minds is the battle between the felines? (*Important note:* Owners wanting to know about cats getting along with dogs, birds and other animals read further. The advice in this chapter can be applied to your version of the problem as well.)

Problems range from mild-mannered cats who turn into fireballs of nastiness when another cat enters the picture to cats who tolerate each other but periodically have serious, knock-down-drag-out fights. There are also the James Dean–type kitties who seem to be okay on the surface but on a deeper level you can tell there's something brewing. It just hasn't happened yet.

How come there are so many fighting cats these days? Why does the fur fly and why, all of a sudden, has this become an issue in the forefront of kitty ownership? The answer is simple: Cat owners are wild about cats! While that may seem like a silly explanation, think about this: Statistics show that the cat population has increased dramatically over the last few decades. But some studies indicate that, although there may be more cats, the percentage of new cat owners may not be rising at the same rate. Some studies go so far as to suggest that there may actually be fewer cat owners. The discrepancy seems to demonstrate that a lot of cat-loving people open their hearts and their homes to a number of cats.

So there are a lot more cats living together than ever before. Those of us who are cat crazy aren't content owning just one, it takes two or more to keep us happy. Others of us feel guilty leaving one cat home alone all by its kitty lonesome.

Visions of two or more cats living happily ever after are often shattered when the pets take an instant dislike to each other. Listening to a stray cat fight under your bedroom window at 4:00 A.M. is one thing, but you haven't lived until you've experienced those same screaming sounds within the confines of your own four walls. The dream of an owner blessed with an adorable cat and kitten family can quickly turn into a case of cats and owner living miserably ever after.

FIGHTING LIKE CATS AND DOGS

Some die-hard pet lovers want the best of all possible worlds. They want a cat in their lives but they also want a dog in their home, maybe even a bird or some fish for good measure. Combining these little critters under one roof conjures up thoughts of dogs making hors d'oeuvres out of fuzzy little kitties; cute Kitty scratching out Fido's eyes; Killer Kitty staking out the bird cage; or even fishing Kitty, complete with fishing rod and reel, vacationing in front of the tank.

It doesn't have to be that way. When properly introduced, cats living together under one roof can learn to be best friends and so can cats and dogs, cats and birds, cats and fish, and even cats and mice. It's simply a matter of negotiating their differences and desensitizing the offending pet to its housemate. The steps given below, while designed to encourage cats to get along, can be applied to all the various pets you want Kitty to learn to love.

THE GREAT BIG BOO-BOO

Pet owners make their biggest mistake by just plunking down the new pet into Kitty's space. In fact, any instant addition to the family may be enough to upset the balance in a cat's life. To gain a better perspective, give some thought as to how you would feel if someone moved into your home on a long-term basis. Suddenly life is different: schedules change, the food in the refrigerator starts to reflect someone else's tastes, and privacy within your own home just isn't what it used to be. Any newly married couple can attest to the changes brought about by cohabitation. However, the newlyweds are adult human beings. Presumably they're mature, capable of rationalizing those differences. They should be prepared to cope with the stress that might surface when dealing with personality conflicts brought about by married life. But it's not news to anyone, as demonstrated by the high rate of divorce, that adult humans don't do very well living together under one roof—and we shouldn't think that the feline animal will be miraculously different.

I believe there are many similarities between child psychology and pet psychology. Think about it. Young children and pets are both sensitive animals who haven't yet figured out our complex world. They're also capable of experiencing many of the same basic emotions. In their naiveté they tend to see things differently from adults. That's why I believe a situation I experienced as a kid allows me to closely identify with pets when they feel their space is infringed upon.

When I was a little boy, both my aunt and uncle died, leaving two young children who needed care. One of those children, a girl about my age, came to live with my family. As I look back on things now, she was a lovely little girl suffering her own pain and sense of confusion at having lost both parents at a very young age. But while it was happening I was terribly upset, jealous of this new kid that had suddenly landed in my home, usurping the attention and affection from my parents that I thought should have been reserved just for my sister and me.

I realize now that I was just too young to really understand what my cousin was going through. At the time, because of all the attention she received and because I felt pushed aside, there was just no way I was going to like her. Having lived through those years, I understand the gamut of emotions that one animal feels when a second animal is thrown all at once into the picture.

There's a basic principle here that many people have come to understand through their own experiences with friends, bosses, and family members (just think of all those mother-in-law jokes). Any two or more animals, whether human, feline, canine, or whatever, spending any great amount of time together are bound to run into problems and differences of opinion. The final result depends on the way things are approached.

NEUTRAL TURF

The words "neutral turf" are not uncommon to any teenage rowdy who, with his equally rowdy companions, could safely meet opposing gangs there—in an area that doesn't belong to either of the groups. Because neither gang is in charge of that territory and since none of the members lives in the neutral zone, there's no need to be protective of the land. It's perceived as a safe place for them to conduct their hooligan business with one another. If, on the other hand, one gang shows up unannounced in the other's territory the odds are good that there will be fighting and possible bloodshed. The group whose neighborhood is invaded feels threatened and perceives a real need to protect themselves, their homes and their loved ones. It may sound like West Side Story but there's a lot of validity to that classic movie—males do challenge one another for superiority. Although it's not an exclusively male problem, the odds of females presenting the same challenge are much less. So, for the purposes of this chapter Kitty is a boy.

A perfectly happy, well-adjusted cat living comfortably in his perfectly normal home may feel a lot like one of those gang members when another cat arrives unannounced. Wham! With no preparation at all, this perfectly happy, well-adjusted cat has the rug pulled out from underneath him. It happens all at once and without any early warning system.

So, with this in mind, you can substantially reduce the risk of trouble if your cats are introduced to each other on neutral turf. If possible, arrange to bring your cat to a friend's home so he can meet his future housemate. Let them check each other out for a few minutes, then take Kitty home alone. Follow up this meeting with several play sessions on neutral territory, always taking Kitty home alone. When the cats seem to be really enjoying each other's company, make arrangements for the big day when the new cat comes home with his "old buddy." *Voilà*, everyone's in one home and happy to be there.

I can feel a lot of you shaking your heads and saying, "This is a whole lot of work. Is he kidding or what?" Well, you'll get no argument from me that this takes a bit of effort, but I can assure you it takes a whole lot less time than dealing with an aggression problem later. An ounce of prevention goes a long, long way.

SEPARATE BUT EQUAL TIME

It's only natural that everyone will want to coo over the new cat once he comes home, but try not to do that in front of your other cat. Save your special attention for private times, setting aside a few five-minute sessions each day alone with each pet. Prevent jealousy by having somebody take one of the pets elsewhere before you do all that private smooching. If that can't be arranged, put the other pet in a large, closed-off room with all sorts of extraordinarily special treats and goodies to help occupy him. Also, turn up the volume of a TV or radio in that room to help drown out your cooing over the other cat.

IT'S PARTY TIME!

Make it seem that wonderful things happen to cat #1 whenever cat #2 is on the scene. Exaggerate everything so this new life-style, complete with new housemate, seems to be great fun—full of goodies, treats, hugs, and kisses. Everytime cat #1 is around cat #2 there should be such a wonderful, major fuss that she thinks you're throwing a party just for her. If medium-cooked roast beef is your cat's favorite thing in the world give her some when the other cat is around. Make her feel like she's just won the million-dollar lottery. I call this the party-time association. Cats learn by association, and if they associate their togetherness with such fabulous fringe benefits, it will help them realize that life's been a blast ever since they met. Never will pet #1 see pet #2 as an intruder. Instead, they will begin to see each other as catalysts for a good time.

Next, be sure there are plenty of toys so that neither cat becomes possessive over playthings. Plenty of playthings doesn't mean five or six, but a couple of dozen. Forcing cats to vie over a few precious toys is bound to bring out their worst sides; it's a perfect way to create aggression. Too few toys may also encourage one cat to bother the other out of sheer boredom.

During the "honeymoon period," when the cats are first getting to know one another, there should be so many toys scattered all over the place that, if you get up in the middle of the night and don't almost kill yourself on all the stuff around, you're doing something wrong. Seriously, there should be all sorts of things thrown about to occupy the cats' attention at any given moment. A cat that's thinking of being feisty or rowdy (or worse, nasty) isn't going to say to himself, "Oh, wait. I don't really want to behave like this. I think I'll wander down the hallway, past the bedroom, through the kitchen and into the den where I can play with my toys instead." Kitty simply won't do that. More than likely he'll annoy the other cat. But if there are all sorts of goodies waiting to distract Kitty, the chances of a fight are greatly diminished.

Remember: During the "getting to know you" stage, frequently change all the play items you've bought for them. It will help keep things interesting. I suggest you add, subtract, change, and rotate as many toys as your wallet allows. Also, be sure to take advantage of all those free things cats love, like paper bags and cardboard boxes (see page 115).

THE DIRTY TOILET PROBLEM

Don't expect your cat to welcome another cat into his litter box with open arms (or should I say paws?). Place a second litter box a reasonable distance from the first box. Be sure to offer cat #1 the same amount of privacy to which he's become accustomed. It's also a good idea to anticipate that someone's going to forget his or her potty habits during the adjustment process. It doesn't hurt to place a few extra boxes around to help ward off the problem. The name of this game is anticipating behavioral problems and taking evasive action before there's a full-scale problem.

THE CHARLES BRONSON SYNDROME

Some cats develop a personality trait I call the Charles Bronson syndrome. You know the type. A bully. He's the cat who, if he had his choice, would be wearing a black leather jacket. This cat decides, in no uncertain terms, that no other cat is going to live in his space under any circumstances, period, the end. This is the cat with whom you must negotiate and be prepared to take things step-by-step.

The first point to consider is that this cat can't—or won't—tolerate *anything* about a new cat companion. You'll need to begin with one little piece of the puzzle at a time. Record a friend's talkative cat or buy a sound-effects record containing cat cries and meows. Play the recording at a very low volume for a few days or weeks until Kitty shows no reaction. Then increase the volume for a few more days or weeks until the cat seems unperturbed by it. Continue the process until the recording is playing at full blast and Charlie Bronson doesn't seem to mind.

The next step is to bring home a few items that contain the odors of the new cat. Leave them around for Kitty to find. Replace them every few days with new items that carry a stronger, fresh scent. During this process, apply the "Party Time" advice I gave on page 80. This will allow the tough-guy cat to slowly get used to the smells and sounds he views as competitive without becoming overwhelmed by the real thing. If you're concerned that Kitty may become really vicious, introduce a stuffed animal that resembles a real cat as much as possible and has been around a real cat so that it has picked up its scent. Play the taped meows at the same time. By creating conditions that simulate a cat before the new cat's arrival, the risk factor of serious fighting later is effectively reduced.

As described earlier, the cats should be introduced on neutral turf. Later, when you bring the new cat home, be sure to install a very tall pet gate, or place one gate on top of another, high enough so that neither cat can jump over it. You'll have to be more creative for those cats with a great deal of climbing expertise. Shore up any openings at the top of the gate or try using a screen door, as long as the bottom is also screened, so tough-guy Kitty can't terrorize the other cat. Since we certainly expect hostility, let them live on opposite sides of the gate or door for a while. Allow them to see and sniff each other while you continue to use all the other steps for "first kitty psychology" previously described. Don't worry if at first they hiss, snarl, and compete for your attention. These four-legged feline kids may behave just like jealous two-legged human kids. But, gradually, and it might be *very slowly,* the game will get old and they'll start to forget about each other.

When things seem safe, and behavior around the gate has been calm for a few weeks, take down the gate for a little while each day. Be sure the cats are securely restrained by a leash and harness (see page 127). By controlling the cats on leashes you'll allow them more freedom and also simulate a more normal household environment without allowing them so much freedom that they run amok. Unfortunately, the bad news is that all the hissing and snarling that ended weeks before may begin again as you embark on the next step of the process. It may seem a bit like Monopoly—when you get the card that says "Go directly to jail. Do not pass go." It is a bit depressing but don't be discouraged. The hissing and snarling will run its course again and slowly disappear. It's helpful to remember that whenever you're dealing with a serious cat behavioral problem there's bound to be ups and downs on the progress scale. Know that it's normal and be reassured that the cats are behaving in the expected manner.

STAY CALM AND DON'T JUMP IN TOO FAST
When pets are learning to adjust to each other it sometimes sounds like an exploding bomb. When this happens, owners need to be careful not to interfere too quickly. Often, what

looks and sounds serious is simply your pets getting to know each other. Interfering can make them feel there is something really intense going on and may actually create the aggression problem you're looking to avoid.

Just when do you butt in? This is one of the hardest judgment calls for owners to make. If you break things up too early you run the risk of contributing to the problem. If you wait too long you may be encouraging a serious fight. Since each cat varies greatly in its personality and temperament, there's no easy answer. Try to be very observant of each cat's body language: the position of the ears, dilation of the pupils, and twitching of the tail (see page 40). Let things go as long as you can, but separate the cats before any of these signs become overly exaggerated. Of course, when in doubt, don't take chances. It's better to break things up too soon than to make a mistake and have an attack take place.

PATIENCE IS A CAT EDUCATOR'S VIRTUE

I'm always amazed when people contact me and say they've tried everything I've suggested and had no results. When I ask how long they've been following my advice, inevitably I hear answers that deal in weeks. It may have been two or three weeks before they threw in the towel. I then ask them how long and how many tries it took for them to quit smoking or shed those extra pounds. (I know about those particular things because I failed miserably on both counts before I finally succeeded.) The point is that it can take time to break bad habits.

While it's true that many of my clients experience immediate (or almost immediate) results with many of their pets' problems, and while this makes me look like the greatest cat expert that ever walked the face of the earth, the truth of the matter is you should consider yourself very lucky if things fall into place right away. It's only reasonable to assume that behavior, particularly those habits that have been ingrained in a cat's personality over a period of months or years, may take some time to change. How long will it take? That's hard to say. So much is determined by the individual cat and what his personal experiences have been. Think of it as therapy. How long does it take someone to resolve deep-rooted psychological problems? Some people do quite well and make dramatic improvements quickly, while others need a therapy support system for years. Fortunately, cats rarely take that long. Nonetheless, many owners tend to be impatient, giving up just before a major breakthrough.

Aggressive, nasty behavior may take the longest of any problem to rectify. Keep at it and you'll more than likely be pleased with the results. Feisty, fighting felines may never become bosom buddies, but the odds are better than 90 percent they'll at least learn to tolerate each other and maintain some form of household harmony.

But don't be surprised if something magical takes place. One day, when you least expect it, you'll walk in and catch your pets snoozing together, nose-to-nose, cuddled up ever so close—friends for life.

SEX AND THE SINGLE CAT

The rendezvous was arranged. All the romantic details were worked out. He was dark and handsome and breathless. She waited in anticipation, her golden red hair shimmering in the sunlight. They were both shy and inexperienced. She stood nervously, hopelessly unable to look at him. She wanted to stare lovingly into his large, soulful eyes, but she couldn't. All she could do was stare at her feet, all four of them.

She and he are pedigreed Persians, brought together for a union that would hopefully bear the fruits of their loving experience, a litter of adorable kittens. But when the big day arrived, neither cat knew what to do; they were willing but didn't have a clue.

Questions about your pets' sexuality don't end with wanting to know about breeding pedigreed cats. Owners have loads of questions about their pets' sexuality, but they're afraid to ask. Now you don't have to—the answers are here.

THE BEST SEX IS NO SEX

The most important rule for sex and the single cat is that there should be no sex. There is a massive overpopulation problem that requires the killing of millions of healthy pets each year—for no other reason than lack of homes. According to *conservative* estimates, in just seven years one cat and her offspring can produce 420,000 kittens. Multiply that by a few extra years and the numbers boggle the mind. I've cried more than a few tears and saved more than a few cats from the shelters' death chambers, even though I realize that no one individual or group of people can drastically reduce those numbers. If you've ever walked the halls of an animal shelter and seen all those little paws reaching out from behind their prison bars, just begging for a little touch, you'll understand my concern. If you've never had the experience, try it. I guarantee it will break your heart, but it may encourage your help in solving the problems that have created the mass murder that takes place with unwanted cats.

CAN KITTY BE A HOMOSEXUAL?

This is a very popular question and the answer isn't what people expect. Many types of animals show homosexual tendencies while still having a heterosexual preference. Some experts think man is one of the few animals that suppresses these tendencies. While it's true that cats will occasionally show an interest in cats of the same sex, very often they're demonstrating dominant behavior as a form of power play. It's usually not sexually related.

MOUNTING, OR WHAT'S LESS
TASTEFULLY CALLED HUMPING

One of the most embarrassing aspects of a pet's sexuality is mounting.

My all time favorite mounting story has to do with two former clients of mine, comedian Rodney Dangerfield and his pet Keno. I was called in to resolve a housetraining problem that had Rodney's pet relieving herself all over his New York City apartment with the final straw coming about because the pet's puddles had actually shorted out his very elaborate and expensive exercise bicycle. While I was there I had the luxury of hearing a Dangerfield classic. Rodney confided to me that a mounting problem was also taking place. And in his trademark style he said, "Talk about no respect—my pet closes her eyes before she mounts my leg."

I see mounting, or humping, much more frequently in dogs, but cats are certainly not exempt. To put this as delicately as possible, mounting takes place when a pet physically attaches itself to an item carrying a strong human odor, often a pillow or bathrobe; jumps sexually on another pet; or becomes attached to someone's leg, usually that of a guest, almost always at the most inappropriate time. It seems that pets have an uncanny knack for humiliating their owners in front of the boss or a new date.

Although mounting is sometimes a sexual response, it very often has more to do with dominant behavior than anything else; it's a simple display of who's the boss. We human animals view it strictly in sexual terms, but the animal kingdom sees it in terms of power and control.

If mounting is a constant problem with your cat, more frequent exercise sessions, more mental stimulation and the teaching of basic commands such as *no* will help control the behavior. Constant mounting may also be a red flag that you're misguiding Kitty in your day-to-day teaching approach.

Can mounting be helped by neutering or spaying? Sometimes yes and sometimes no, but I never count on surgery to correct possible behavioral problems. Since the subject of altering (neutering and spaying) a cat is confusing to some Kitty owners, I've expanded on it later in this chapter.

CAN KITTY BE A NYMPHOMANIAC?

"Oh come on now!" you're saying. "This sounds like the title of a bad TV talk show trying to get good rating points." Nevertheless, a female Kitty *can* be a nymphomaniac, a problem brought about by excessive hormone production (*hyperestrinism* is the medical term). A similar problem can also occur with males (*satyriasis*). Males and females could have an increased interest in riding, or mounting, *anything*. Kitty could also have a Jekyll and Hyde personality—getting nasty at peak points. Veterinarians can usually treat this problem, and neutering or spaying is often recommended.

NYMPHOMANIA VS. CONSTANT HEAT

"Oh no! Not more on nymphomania!" you're saying. Well, not quite. At times, something occurs with the lady cats that some owners call constant heat. Kitty looks as if she's in heat and shows a lot of the symptoms. It seems to go on all the time, or at least way too long, and male cats are much too interested in her. If this happens to your young lady, have her checked by the vet. Surgery may be required.

STRANGE BUT TRUE

One of the most interesting points about sex and the single cat is that if left to live outdoors, an unspayed female cat's heat cycle is often inactive during the colder months. The cycle is then brought on by longer daylight hours, which begin in springtime and seem to have a significant effect on her hormones. It's Mother Nature's way of ensuring that the litter is born during the warmer months, with a better chance of survival. I always find these sorts of things amazing—how, in the scheme of things, nature provides for its own. On the other hand, indoor cats' heat cycles are often fooled by our technologically temperature-controlled environments. Heats can then be as frequent as every fifteen to twenty-one days and may continue for approximately nine to ten days if mating doesn't take place.

EVEN STRANGER BUT STILL TRUE

Did you know that one litter of kittens can have more than one father? A female cat can have more than one mate during her heat cycle and these different males can father one or more of the kittens in the very same litter.

FALSE PREGNANCY

The old saying "There's no such thing as being a little bit pregnant" doesn't quite hold true for some pets. There is a "sort of " pregnancy that can occur at any time, even when no male has been involved. More commonly seen in dogs, occasionally a cat will suffer a false pregnancy. These are often brought on by a hormonal imbalance, although I've seen a few that were purely psychological.

False pregnancies are just that—false. Kitty's not actually pregnant but shows many of the medical or emotional signs that she might be. In its mildest form, a cat will "nest" with some of her favorite toys or owner's personal belongings, treating them like kittens. An owner's fuzzy slippers or cuddly, soft sweaters, or the kids' stuffed animals might disappear. They'll often turn up piled in a corner behind a chair, wet and yucky from the confused mama cat licking and nurturing them. When it's more serious, there are physical signs, including swelling of the abdomen. Some vets let the mild form simply run its course with no real intervention. With more serious cases, medications and spaying are sometimes the suggested solutions. In strictly psychological cases, I've seen a number of cats and dogs exhibit signs of false pregnancy even after spaying. When dealing with behavior, anything is possible.

THE ULTIMATE FORM OF
BIRTH CONTROL—
SPAYING AND NEUTERING

Any kitty that might get together with cats of the opposite sex, no matter how fluffy and adorable you may think he or she is, should be neutered or spayed. The only exception should be pedigreed cats that are extraordinary representatives of their breeds. My feelings on this subject run deep and strong. The massive killing of healthy, homeless pets each year has gotten out of hand. As far as I'm concerned, indiscriminate breeding is a cardinal sin.

Neutering is the term generally used for altering, or castrating, males. Spaying, a type of hysterectomy, is the term used for females. In addition to removing the ability to breed, spaying and neutering are considered by some health professionals as a means to lessen the incidence of cancer of the reproductive system. A lesser known alternative, one that is not widely practiced but is available, is vasectomies for males, which sterilizes them but leaves them physically and sexually intact.

WILL FIXING KITTY CREATE
BETTER BEHAVIOR?

Neutering and spaying are often suggested as a means of resolving pet behavioral problems and calming a hyperactive personality. However, I don't always agree. Neutering or spaying are not magic wands for dealing with problems of behavior! Cats should be neutered and spayed for reasons of health and birth control. Behavioral problems, particularly when they've developed into well-established habits, should be dealt with by a training and behavioral therapy program. For instance, a male cat's indiscriminate urinating, once begun, may not be helped by neutering alone.

MISCONCEPTIONS ABOUT SPAYING AND NEUTERING

The big misconception is that cats, once they're spayed or neutered, become fat and lazy. Only those owners with a heavy hand on the can opener who provide too much food and too little exercise can create a grossly out-of-shape pet.

Spaying and neutering will not negatively affect the looks and personality of a pet. Once a gorgeous cat always a gorgeous cat.

A female does not need to be bred at least once. It is also not a good idea to allow her to have one litter in order for your children to witness the miracle of birth.

WHEN'S THE BIG DAY?

Veterinarians differ on exactly what age cats should be spayed or neutered, but most agree that it should be done within the first year, and there is a growing trend toward neutering and spaying at very early ages. However, if your cat is older, the operation can certainly still be performed, providing Kitty is healthy enough for surgery. Simply check with your vet.

BIRTH-CONTROL ALTERNATIVES

If you have personal reasons for not spaying or neutering your cat, then adhere to the next best form of birth control—a leash (see page 121). No unaltered cat should be allowed to run free—you'll just be contributing to the tragedy of the overpopulation problem. You should also, of course, keep Kitty away from cats of the opposite sex that live in your home. There are products available through veterinarians that can help delay a heat cycle, but they're generally recommended for short-term use only.

OOPS! WHAT ARE THOSE SIX TINY THINGS ALL CUDDLED UP IN THE BACK OF THE CLOSET?

Should an unwanted pregnancy take place, a veterinarian can terminate it in its early stages. If personal beliefs prevent you from having a pregnancy terminated or, if by some mystery, there's a litter of kitties you didn't know anything about, you should be responsible for that litter. That doesn't mean dumping the little kitties off at the local overcrowded and under-funded humane society. The litter is *your* responsibility. Care for them. Then locate good, loving homes for each defenseless kitten. And please get that cat spayed!

IF YOU'RE DEAD SET ON BREEDING . . .

Only cats of exceptional pedigree quality, falling well within the written standards for that breed as outlined by one of the several pedigree cat registries and deemed excellent by a pro-fessional cat-show judge, should be considered for breeding purposes. Some of the registry organizations may help you locate a good mate, but generally only owners of proven cham-pions will be encouraged to breed their cats.

Pets should be fully mature before breeding. Opinions def-initely vary on when a pet is mature. I personally think it is two years of age, sometimes older. Many cats who are younger than that are either physically or emotionally juvenile, neither of which is the best criterion for good parenting.

One of the two partners should be experienced. Although two amateurs may be interested in each other, they may not be able to figure out exactly what they need to do. In that case, it's up to the owners to literally get in the act—you'll have to help demonstrate all the right moves. Kitty's sexual instruction is certainly something not all owners want to put on their "things to do'' list. Most owners don't want their daily chores to include picking up the dry cleaning, stopping at the store for bread, and helping Kitty with her sex life.

If all goes well between the two kitties, the female's appetite will increase and so will the size of her belly. Approximately fifty-nine to sixty-eight days later, give or take a few, there should be a litter of highly adorable kittens.

Don't shy away from asking your vet questions about Kitty's sexuality—there's nothing to be afraid of. And understanding it will make Kitty's life happier and healthier.

5

❖   ❖   ❖

KITTY
KINDERGARTEN

START KITTY'S EDUCATION
EARLY

As soon as Kitty comes into your life she's ready for the at-home version of Kitty Kindergarten. Make it fun and don't overly structure anything. Guide her gently in the right direction. Don't use any corrections, but give her lots of praise and love instead.

Some people will certainly argue with me on this point. Many experts suggest waiting until Kitty's older, but I believe that when she's old enough to get into the garbage, she's old enough to learn *not* to get into it. When Clint "Kitty" Eastwood is old enough to hold the dog hostage, she's old enough to learn how to be friends instead. When she knows how to keep us chasing after her until we give up, she's old enough to begin her education. After all, she just outsmarted us, didn't she?

The earlier she's introduced to things in a fun way, the less traumatic it will be for her to learn later on. This type of early training also develops a certain self-confidence. She'll be able to strut around and say, "Hey, this is no big deal."

The only exception to this early educational program involves excursions to the great outdoors. Check with the vet to determine when Kitty's vaccinations will give her enough protection to go outside.

THE LITTER BOX PROBLEM

True or false: All cats find their way to the litter box—it's instinctive.

The answer is false, but don't feel bad if you didn't answer the question correctly. You're simply one of many people who have been misled. If you answered "false," the odds are you're familiar with the embarrassment that comes from having a home that smells like a horse stable. You've probably also become an expert on cleaning products that eliminate every odor known to man *except* for one—the odor of cat urine. Yes, I can see all you cleaning *mavens* out there nodding your heads.

The question I'm most frequently asked by owners is how they can keep their cats from ignoring the litter box, either all or part of the time. These owners are desperate. Nothing's worse than an untrained cat who chooses any part of the home, other than the litter box, as his bathroom. This Kitty thinks on a grand scale—your home is one great big toilet built especially for him.

ALL LITTER BOX PROBLEMS
ARE NOT THE SAME

Litter box problems take a variety of directions. Fussy kitties use the litter box most of the time, having only occasional accidents on the floor. Others are in the on-again-off-again category; it's fifty-fifty with them. Then there are the extremely sensitive cats whose toilet habits can be disrupted by any emotional upheaval or problem within the family, such as a divorce or a new baby. And then there are those cats who just don't have a clue. These cats simply prefer your closet, your best shoe or pocketbook, the middle of the most expensive piece of carpet, or, heaven forbid, your pillow. I know how it is. You have my sympathy.

I'm lucky. Mowdy's a pro when it comes to using the litter box. My little furball is even amazing when he travels with me—I can put down a litter box anytime, anywhere, even in a strange hotel room and he'll use it with no trouble at all. Well, your cat can be like that, too. Any Kitty can learn the finer points of using the box.

BELIEVE IT OR NOT, YOUR CAT PROBABLY ISN'T TRYING TO BE BAD

Flabbergasted by your cat's behavior when she makes a deposit somewhere other than in the litter box? The main thing you need to remember is that 99.9999 times out of 100, cats are *not* spiteful. They really don't stay up late at night thinking of ways to get even with you. They don't lounge around in bed contemplating a list of aggravating, villainous deeds. In virtually every case there is a reason or more likely a combination of reasons that trigger off a response. Nonuse of the litter box is no exception.

THE HANSEL AND GRETEL SYNDROME

If you're wondering why Kitty's little indiscretions occur on your pillow, perhaps when someone in the family is out of town, think about what I have termed the Hansel and Gretel syndrome. Cats, like certain other animals, use their excrement as a means of sending out a message. First, the scent lets other cats know they're coming close to your Kitty's turf. Second, the scent helps attract certain other cats with whom Kitty wishes to mingle. But it also helps kitties to find their way, just like the bread crumbs Hansel and Gretel dropped on their journey through the woods. So, when someone's out of the house and Kitty's missing that family member, she may leave little accidents around as a means of helping her loved one find her way back home, particularly on things that strongly carry the person's scent. From your point of view it may look like intentional spite, because it seems to happen only when you're gone. But if you look at it from Kitty's perspective it takes on a whole new meaning.

WHY THE EXPLOSION OF
LITTER BOX PROBLEMS?

Why is there such an explosion of cat litter box problems? The most obvious answer is that since cats are an attractive choice for today's pet owners, the number of pet cats has risen dramatically. One big reason for their attractiveness is that they're cheap to keep, cheaper than many dogs. They also don't have to be walked after the eleven o'clock nightly news. But with an increase in cats comes an increase in cat behavioral problems. This is partly due to the increase in first-time cat owners. Novice owners just don't have the same working knowledge of cat behavior that their more experienced counterparts, who have survived years of feline shenanigans, do. I'm convinced cats know how to take advantage of rookie owners.

Also, there are more multicat households than ever before—people who own two, three, four, or more cats. This also creates problems. The odds are that, in a bevy of cats in one home, at least one of the group will have some behavioral problem.

Another factor playing a major role in the rise of litter box problems is the two-income family. Household members are simply too busy to teach Kitty the proper toilet training habits. It's understandable—but it doesn't do poor Kitty—or you—any good.

THE BATTLE OF
THE BOXES

Litter box selection is really a matter of what's right for you as well as what's right for Kitty—but the emphasis should be on Kitty's preference. If Kitty doesn't like it, you're finished. Kaput.

A box is a box is a box is how owners generally feel about litter boxes. Wrong again. There are litter boxes that are small and rectangular, large and rectangular, ones with high sides, ones with tops, ones that have charcoal filters and some that even are disposable. If Kitty doesn't like one kind, try another. And keep trying until she approves of one of them.

AN OPEN LITTER BOX IS SOMETIMES TOUGH TO TAKE

Some cats like the wide-open pans, while others prefer their privacy, choosing a covered box. If you prefer a covered litter box but Kitty doesn't, you could still give it a try. During the first week or two, use the pan without the cover, laying the cover near the box. If Kitty's consistently using it after a few weeks, attach the cover—stand it straight up or propped three quarters of the way up. For the next few weeks prop the cover halfway up, then a quarter of the way up. Finally it can be closed all the way. This gives Kitty an idea of what's coming, eliminating any major last minute adjustments.

KITTY SCREENS

Sometimes Kitty looks embarrassed when caught in the act of using the litter box. To help Kitty maintain her modesty, and as a fringe benefit to help hide the unsightly box, try a kitty screen. A kitty screen is a smaller version of the old-fashioned boudoir dressing screens you've seen in Hollywood western movies. You know the kind—there's always a gorgeous woman changing her clothes behind one while a man is in the room.

Kitty screens are available commercially. If you want to be creative, you could even make your own.

THE LITTER DILEMMA

I believe the single most important reason why cats don't use litter boxes is because of the litter itself. Years ago we had very little choice about which litter to use. It was either sand, dirt from the garden, or a basic clay litter available at the pet shop or supermarket. Well, times have changed. Shopping for cat litter today is like going to the fragrance counter at Macy's. We have red litter, green litter, mint odor, evergreen odor, time-activated, chemically controlled, organically controlled, and so many other varieties that it's enough to make a sane man crazy. What to do? What to do?

We have done so much with litter that we have confused our cats right out of their boxes. Bear in mind that cats, like most of us, are creatures of habit. No one told them modern technology dictates that their bathroom litter has to be different. Clearly no one told our little furballs they need to use laboratory-produced litter that smells like a forest, is time released, charcoal filtered, etc., etc. Cats don't want to know from all this. They just want their bathrooms back. Let's face it, we all feel more comfortable in the old familiar john.

Even more important, have you ever smelled some of the new litters? Some of them stink like really bad, cheap after-shave lotion. If this stuff was in my litter box I'd probably have an accident in the laundry room myself. Cats have a very keen sense of smell, much better than our own. I firmly believe that many of the so-called advances and technological break-throughs in kitty litter have caused behavioral setbacks in many of our cats. Only since these modern-day products have hit the market has there been an upsurge in litter box problems. Sometimes the old ways are the best ways.

Don't misunderstand me. If your cat is doing well on one of the new litters, that's fine. Take advantage of the extra benefits of odor control, less dust, and the like. I'm a big believer in the old adage that if it's not broken don't fix it. Your cat may be able to tolerate any type of litter, but if you're discovering little surprises all over the floor, you may find it helps to go back to the basics.

CLEANING CONFUSION AND PIGSTY BOXES

The other major reason cats stop using their litter boxes is plain old dirt. We've all grown up being told cats are fastidiously clean and, in almost every case, that's true. Why then are so many litter boxes changed so infrequently? Many cat owners change the litter once or twice a week at best. The more conscientious ones scoop out the dirty litter a little more often. If you're suffering from the litter box training blues, it may be because you aren't cleaning the box frequently enough.

I'll always remember one of my clients who was the chairman of the board of a Fortune 500 company. He had two cats already in the family when his wife brought home the third. That's when all heck broke loose. The three cats stopped using the litter box. There was urine and stool all over the very luxurious Park Avenue, New York City duplex apartment. One day I received a frantic call from the chairman's wife. Formal dinner parties, a necessity in her husband's position, were out of the question. How could she entertain when the entire apartment reeked from the cats' mistakes?

We set up an appointment for the following day. The building was one of the best addresses in New York City and the apartment was filled with priceless treasures. Now I'm more than accustomed to cat odors, and very strong ones at that, but the stench took my breath away. I could not believe anyone would let a problem go on for so long without trying to do something about it. The problem was severe, but we gave it a whirl.

Many things were wrong: diet, incorrect cleansers, and too many harsh corrections. Most of all, the problem was the litter box itself. So many mounds of bowel movements were sticking up from the litter that at first I thought I was looking at one of the many abstract sculptures gracing their home. No kidding. It was the filthiest, dirtiest box I had ever seen. No wonder the cats weren't using it—they would have deserved a medal just for climbing into it! Put yourself in their place. If you were one of those cats, would you use it? Think about how you feel when you're driving along, desperate for a bathroom, and the only one available is at a sleazy, disgusting gas station. I've known plenty of people who, desperate or not, just won't use facilities in these conditions. And I don't blame them. So why would we think our cats wouldn't prefer the back of the living room couch over their equivalent of a filthy bathroom?

My main suggestion was to have the owners change the litter every day. I also recommended additional litter boxes, including one on the second floor of the apartment to reduce the risk factor for accidents. Some cats, particularly at night, are reluctant to get up from their sleep and walk down a flight of steps in an unlit home just to try to find their box.

I'm happy to say that only days after my visit, the problem had been solved. Although the owners thought I was a miracle worker, and recommended me to many of their friends, I really didn't do anything so special. Common sense dictates that if cats are such clean animals, they may not drag themselves into an unclean litter box, or even a clean one that retains the harsh odor of a household cleaner. No one likes a dirty or smelly bathroom—and that certainly holds true for Kitty.

Some cats are born inherently cleaner than others or develop extra clean habits at some point during their lives. Extra clean or no, all cats should have their litter changed—not just scooped—several times a week. In particular, a cat who is having a litter box training problem should have her box cleaned every day or sometimes twice a day. For those of you sitting there tallying up the cost of extra litter and thinking that in giving you this type of advice my brain must have been affected by breathing in all that cat hair around me, I can only say that contrary to popular opinion you do not have to fill the box with litter. You don't even have to fill it halfway. Most cats will be perfectly content using a box containing just enough litter so they may scratch and cover up their mess. Sometimes less is better.

THE BIG CLEANUP

When accidents occur, a big mistake made by many cat owners is in their choice of a cleaning agent. Almost every good home-maker grabs for a bottle of ammonia or a cleanser that contains ammonia. But, have you ever picked up a baby's dirty diaper after it's been sitting around for too long? *Whew!* that ammonia smell will get to you in no time! Both urine and stool contain a form of ammonia. By cleaning up accidents with ammoniated products, as far as the cat is concerned, you're pouring something on the floor with an odor that is almost identical to the one you're trying to get rid of. You might as well send Kitty a written invitation asking her to return to the scene of the crime. It's like saying, "That's a good cat, go potty over here, and over there by the chair, and under the dining room table, and while you're at it how about doing a little by the bed?" Not a pretty picture, is it?

Avoid the cleanup trap by purchasing a product that is an odor neutralizer (available at better pet shops). These products will actually neutralize the odor through the enzymes or similar reagents it contains. Be sure the product label specifically states that it is a neutralizer. Many products merely mask or cover up the odor for the human's sense of smell but aren't nearly effective enough for Kitty's keener olfactory sense.

Don't assume that a professional carpet-cleaning service is the answer, either. Some of these companies use products that are chosen for their effectiveness in eliminating dirt and odors for human beings. Just because everything smells fine to us, little Kitty still knows where she's been. Always ask what the products contain. Be sure there are no forms of ammonia in the cleaning agent and ask the cleaning professionals if your odor neutralizer can be added to their solution. If the carpet cleaning company will do this, it will save you a lot of time and aggravation.

Shampooing the carpets yourself? Read the labels carefully to be sure the combination of chemicals won't cause a health hazard for you, the cat, or anything else that lives under your roof.

SPECIAL TRICKS TO PREVENT
LITTER BOX MISTAKES

Prevention is better than correction—at least, that's my philosophy about behavior. I'd much rather help a pet circumvent a problem than be corrective, authoritative, punitive, or dominant. I'm much happier developing special little tricks that will ease Kitty out of her bad behavior without her even realizing it. Because there are so many types of litter box questions, I've put together a list so you can better determine which category you and Kitty fall into.

WHAT IF . . .

• *What if #1:* The first "what if" concerns people who want Kitty to use the toilet in the bathroom. I swear to you that I know people who have trained their cats to do this, and over the years I've seen Kitty toilet seats and training aids sold at pet shops. That's not for Mowdy and me. We have a simple agreement: He doesn't use my toilet and I don't use his litter box. I really don't want to have to knock on the bathroom door and wait on line because the cat is inside and temporarily indisposed. Besides, he always forgets to flush. If you want to train Kitty to use your toilet you have my blessings, but think twice about the possible inconvenience.

My all-time favorite cat/bathroom story has to do with Ron Reagan, Jr., and his cat. While working together on a segment for the television show *Good Morning America,* Ron told me that when he lived in one of his previous apartments, the bathroom was right off the living room, so that people seated in the living room had a perfect view of the bathroom door and vice versa. But there was one little hitch. The door didn't close securely and the cat knew it. Whenever someone used the facilities, the cat would wait an appropriate amount of time for the person to settle in, and would then simply walk over and open the door, just in time to let everyone see the guest sitting . . . ah, well, you know where.

What if #2: The second "what if " takes place when the new kitten doesn't *know* what a litter box box is, doesn't *care* what a litter box is, and mother nature seems to have given Kitty no other instinct about toilet training other than wherever she happens to be is good enough. Begin by thinking small. Gate or block off a small area, approximately five feet by five feet. Place a clean litter box at one end. Scatter toys all over the space, and keep food and water dishes at the other end. Whenever you can't watch little Kitty, confine her in this area. But don't overdo the confinement. Use it only when you can't watch her carefully and make sure she can't hurt herself if she tries to get out. Because the remaining sections of the floor are covered, she will have no choice but to climb into the litter box, choosing not to do her business in her dishes or on top of her playthings. Also, place a drop of ammonia mixed with water at the bottom of the box to help attract Kitty and so the familiar odor helps to trigger the correct behavioral response.

Important: The key is to confine that fleet-footed little bundle of fur. Kittens are quick. In no time they're gone and out of your line of sight. Don't be suckered into relaxing; cats will outsmart you every time if you are. Be 100 percent consistent and you'll be able to gradually expand her enclosed area, a little at a time every few days, as she becomes trustworthy. If you become sloppy and let her have a few accidents here and there, nothing will be accomplished other than to delay the progress and lengthen the period of time she is restricted. Stick to the program and in no time you'll be cleaning out the litter box just like the rest of us.

• *What if #3:* Has the furball decided that certain areas of the house are her preferred elimination spots? Kitties who select a few favorite spots for mistakes are the most common litter box offenders. Most cats will pick out one to three different areas where they prefer to soil. In the most severe cases, there may be half a dozen hot spots. Only after you've kept the litter box immaculately clean and checked the brand of litter and the cleaning agent/odor neutralizer should you take this next step. If you begin this procedure prematurely it may have no effect at all other than to encourage the cat to pick out yet more places in the house to soil.

To repeat a point that I made before, we've all heard how cats like to be clean. Always licking and grooming themselves, they rarely fail to wash after every meal. Because nature built this clean factor into a cat's psyche, one of the easiest ways to prevent a cat from soiling outside the litter box is to begin feeding Kitty in those areas where accidents take place. Cats *hate* to eliminate around their feeding areas.

To do this, divide Kitty's normal food portions into his regular dish and onto several paper plates. You should have one paper plate for each area being soiled. For example, if the cat's favorite areas for elimination are in the bathtub (a favorite spot for many cats), in the pantry and on top of the dirty laundry pile, you should divide the meal into four parts. The regular feeding bowl should be left at its normal location and should contain one quarter of the meal. The remaining food should be divided into three additional parts. One plate should be placed in the pantry, another on the laundry pile, and the other into the bathtub. If you think it sounds disgusting to have these food dishes in places like the tub, I guarantee it's better than the alternative. Don't pick up the paper plates when Kitty finishes the food, but leave them there as reminders. Continue this process for a few weeks.

Once Kitty has demonstrated he has broken his old habit, remove a plate for a day and then put it back in place. Wait a few days. Repeat that process a few times. When two or three weeks go by with no accidents, completely remove one of the plates. Wait a week. If there are still no lapses of bad behavior, remove the second plate. Wait a week. If everything's okay, remove the third and so forth. Should Kitty suffer a regression and again soil in those hot spots it simply means you moved too quickly. Backtrack and start over, remaining at each stage for a longer period of time. You have nothing to lose by moving ahead too slowly and everything to lose by moving too quickly.

Try placing sheets of aluminum foil over hot spot areas if food dishes can't be used. Some cats don't like the sound or feel of walking on aluminum foil.

- *What if #4:* How do you limit the confusion of an outdoor cat who must now learn to live indoors? An indoor environment can be very strange for cats that have become adjusted to having the great outdoors as their bathroom. To help ease Kitty into the adjustment, try using dirt (or sand, if that's what most closely resembles the old outdoor bathroom) in the litter box. After a few weeks, when the cat seems to be getting adjusted, gradually change to indoor litter—but this must be done gradually. For example, if the litter has been made up of dirt, change the consistency to 75 percent dirt and 25 percent litter for several weeks. If all goes well, make another change to 50 percent dirt and 50 percent litter. Then, a few weeks later, change to 75 percent litter and 25 percent dirt, and then just to litter.

- *What if #5:* When an older kitty forgets herself, there are probably more than a few senior-citizen-type problems creating the lapse in behavior. Golden-year kitties are special and I have a separate little spot in my heart just for them.

They've given us the best years of their lives and the least we can do is give them extra care when they need it most. For this reason I've devoted an entire section to senior citizen cats (see page 200). Please refer to it for the old-timers' litter box needs as well as for advice on how to make their remaining time with us happy and healthy.

PRAISING KITTY

Praise, praise, praise Kitty for every positive step she takes. The instant she's done what she's supposed to do in the box, go overboard with praise. Exaggerate all sorts of wonderful phrases. Tell her she's wonderful, how pleased you are, and how she's the best thing that ever walked on four legs. Hug her. Pet her. Love her. Carry on like an idiot for a couple of minutes. With all this positive attention flying in her direction, Kitty's bound to pick up on what you're asking. No quick pats on the head accompanied by blasé praise. Accentuate the positive. Let Kitty think she's a star.

IF YOU MUST CORRECT THE CAT . . .

As I said before, I'm not a fan of using corrections to change behavior. However, as a last resort, try leaving the cat with its accident. Confine the cat in a small area with its urine or stool. Urine may be soaked up on a paper towel and the towel placed with Kitty. Leave the cat with its mess for twenty minutes *only,* coming back at two ten-minute intervals to say *no.* Say "no" and only "no." Don't recite a whole speech about how upset you are and how he should wait until Daddy gets home. Too much attention to the problem is just as bad as not enough. At the end of the twenty minutes, stop. Forget about it, and don't hold any grudges.

By making Kitty stay with his mess, you're telling him: "I don't care where you go in the house. If you make a mistake, you're just going to stay with it." It's like sending a kid to his room for twenty minutes to think about something wrong he said or did. With Kitty, the only difference is that you're putting the accident with him to help remind him what he should be thinking about.

Don't rub his nose in it. That's humiliating. Don't bring him over to the spot and yell at him. All you're doing is telling him it's bad to go there in that particular spot. The next day he'll move a little to the left and go over there, then move a little to the right and go over there.

SOME WORDS FOR MORAL SUPPORT

Generally speaking, the longer any habit has been in existence, the more time is needed to correct it. It really has nothing to do with the age of the cat or any other factor except for the length of time the problem has been a *habit*. The more ingrained the behavior, the longer it usually takes to reverse the procedure.

Whatever you do, don't become frustrated if Kitty suffers one or more relapses. This is normal to the learning process. Just because everything is going along famously and you've patted yourself on the back for a job well done and then suffered a setback, don't give up! This is perfectly okay. Regressions should be expected. We often fail in our first, second, or third attempts to modify our behavior. However, in each case we come away having learned something that adds greatly to the possibility of success the next time around. The same principle applies to our bundles of fur when they're learning something new or kicking an old bad habit.

SCRATCHING, CLAWING, AND THE GENERAL DESTRUCTION OF HOUSEHOLD POSSESSIONS

Are you tired of your home looking like a war zone? Has Kitty picked out a favorite easy chair—not for sleeping but for scratching? Have you decided you can't continue spending your paycheck repairing Kitty's damage as she redecorates and redesigns the furniture by scratching and clawing it? If your home has all the telltale signs of cougars, lions, and tigers roaming about when all you own is a tiny tabby, this section of the book is for you. It's amazing that such little animals can do so much damage. Ten pounds of cuteness and fluff really can turn an entire home upside down and drive a grown person to tears.

You know you have the beginning of trouble when you find mysterious little marks on your walls, generally around corner moldings, or when small pieces of Sheetrock miraculously appear on the floor. You know you've graduated to big trouble when furniture stuffing clings to the little darling's paws as she walks nonchalantly around the house.

If this describes the situation with your little warrior, you don't need me to tell you that your cat has a scratching, clawing, or even chewing problem. (Yes, some cats do chew.) Your home will speak for itself. Suddenly the well-decorated home develops a bargain-basement look. Throw blankets show up on furniture everywhere in your valiant, but futile, attempt to hide the damage. It makes no difference where you live. Cat owners from Beverly Hills to Brooklyn, from Paris to Peoria, have little blankets that confirm, to those of us who know about these things, that there's a cat in the house who just can't keep her hands, or paws, to herself.

Whenever I give advice on cat scratching and destruction I always have to fight off the giggles. It's not that I find these things so funny. Certainly I have sympathy for all owners living in a bomb zone. It's just that it always reminds me of a know-it-all lawyer who was a client of mine. First, I'd like to make it clear that as a rule I find attorneys make wonderful pet owners. When dealing with pet problems, lawyers are usually extremely fair. I think it has something to do with their knowledge of negotiations and compromise—they don't expect to have it all their way. But this lawyer was different. He knew better than everyone about everything. When his six-month-old calico kitten started clawing the back of his favorite easy chair, his wife ran into the room to correct the cat. "No, no dear," he said in his standard, condescending voice. "That's not how to do it. Show Kitty she's wrong by putting her outside. That will teach her."

Each time the cat clawed the chair the lawyer put the cat outside to reinforce his learning technique. Well, the cat certainly did learn. Calico Kitty learned that every time she wanted to go outside to play she simply had to wander over and scratch the chair. The wife, who is sweet as punch, eventually took my advice and ironed out all this nonsense with the cat. But her husband still doesn't get it. He's sure his way is still the best way.

WHY DO CATS SCRATCH AND CLAW?

Let's do a little Kitty psychoanalysis. By putting Kitty "on the couch" we can see that her destructive behavior has nothing to do with spite. To get a better handle on scratching and clawing, it's important to understand the origins of the behavior. Only then can we deal with and channel incorrect responses.

First, most cats need to claw and scratch. They scratch for a variety of reasons, primarily to stretch and exercise, trim their nails, reduce stress, as well as for a little known and less understood reason—to leave behind their scent in much the same way males urinate to mark their turf.

THE BIG BOMB: BOREDOM

When we further analyze Kitty, we'll often find that the biggest contributor to inappropriate scratching is boredom. In years gone by, cats could wander outdoors, scratching on a tree in one area and clawing on a log in another. The world was a curious place and, from the cats' perspective, made solely for their exploration. When left to their own devices, cats are nomadic. They like to roam around and experience life. Have you ever watched a stray cat explore a new area? Kitty will wander, sniff and climb in, out, and over the most precariously placed items. Most modern-day cats have had this luxury taken away from them.

City living and suburban development have made it unsafe for cats to wander freely around the neighborhood. Now, most pets live in concrete spaces, and life outdoors brings an ever-present threat from traffic. Things just aren't what they used to be. Adventure and outdoor activity are no longer a part of many cats' life-styles. Without new adventures, the effects of insufficient mental and physical stimulation—boredom and complacency—set in, and before you know it . . . there goes the couch.

P-L-E-A-S-E DON'T EVEN THINK ABOUT USING THOSE CRAZY CORRECTIONS

Unfortunately, many owners are advised to correct, punish, yell at, scold, and maybe even hit cats who scratch or destroy things in the home. Certain cat experts are the worst offenders for giving out this type of advice. I'm not quite sure what it is about these people who are attracted to animal training and behavior, but it seems that too many of them actually enjoy "correcting" animals. I think sometimes it has to do with a need to dominate something. It's both horrifying and amazing that harsh methods are endorsed by so many pet and animal advocates—things like spreading Tabasco sauce, hot Chinese mustard, or jalapeño peppers on items that are being chewed.

Then there's the suggestion to squirt the cat with hot water (I've heard of ammonia, too). And have you heard the one about setting mousetraps so when the cat goes near it the trap springs shut, possibly on the cat's paw or tongue? I'm not making these things up. Techniques like these, and worse, can be found in a number of training books. My heart always goes out to loving pet owners who, frustrated by their pet's incorrect behavior, seek help from these "experts." Imagine their chagrin when they hear the cat's first scream or see Kitty running wildly about the house, desperately shaking her head and rubbing her mouth now that the taste of the hot peppers, or a similar substance, took hold. Kitty suffers and the owners never quite forgive themselves for subjecting their beloved furball to such rough treatment.

A KINDER, MORE GENTLE APPROACH
Well, I'm happy to say there are kinder and gentler ways to channel misdirected energy.

My motto in this area is: You can't teach a cat not to scratch or chew, but you can teach Kitty precisely *what* to scratch or chew. It's nature's way. Cats are supposed to trim their nails and stretch their bodies by clawing and scratching. Some are even born with a desire to experiment and taste new things. To try to correct them from doing what Mother Nature intended is to possibly confuse them to the point of even further behavioral problems. Punishing instinctive behavior may create deep-rooted neurosis. It would be like correcting a baby each time it tried to use its hands.

ENTERTAIN YOUR CAT
You might be asking yourself, "If I'm not supposed to correct the cat, just what am I supposed to do?" Set up some Kitty entertainment! People need to get out of the house and make a night of it at the local comedy club or take an exotic trip to Club Med. Well, Kitty can't go wind surfing, but owners can certainly make her life more interesting. The first step is easy yet it's the one most often overlooked. How many playthings does your cat have? Right now, look up from where you're sitting. Scan the room. Better yet, get on your hands and knees and crawl around so you can see it from Kitty's perspective. I bet that, at the most, there are a few old toys around. Their novelty probably wore off months ago. *Boring!*

No cheating, now. Don't even think about telling me there's plenty of stuff around but it all happens to be under the chair or the sofa. The bottom line is that if they're not in the room *now* they don't count. If you can't see the playthings, then you're part of the problem. Be part of the solution instead.

Be sure Kitty has a bundle of toys. That goes for all the owners who say, "But my cat doesn't *like* any toys. She won't play with anything." To this I say, "pooh-pooh." I've yet to find a cat that won't play with something. For all the doubting Thomases, there *are* cats who turn up a disinterested nose at a lot of different playthings, but keep at it. Try everything that is commercially available or anything you can create. I guarantee, in almost every single case, you will come across something the furball enjoys.

I'll never forget the time I was working with one of Lily Tomlin's pets, Tess. Tess had a real aversion to all the normal toys and playthings. I tried an assortment of things to grab Tess's attention, but nothing worked. Believing my reputation was at stake, I walked the streets of Beverly Hills. I remember it was an incredibly hot day and I thought: What the heck am I doing, me, a boy from the Bronx spending his free time on one of his first California trips looking for toys to keep some pet interested. Shouldn't I be enjoying myself at the pool or doing something else instead? *Anything* else? But *noooo!* I was walking the streets looking for pet toys! Finally, I came across the answer in a children's store. It was something called a Superball—which bounced high and erratically. First it bounced to the right, then it took off to the left, then it landed unpredictably before taking a backward hop, followed by a quick turn to the front. You just couldn't anticipate where it would go.

Well, this sparked Tess's interest. Because she was particularly bright and clever, she had found the typical, standard toys rather mundane—but how she enjoyed the challenge of the Superball! In order to play with it she had to stay on her toes. It held her attention and saved my reputation. I will always be indebted to that bouncy rubber ball.

No matter how aloof or detached you think your cat may be,

more than likely there are toys and activities she'll enjoy. However, sometimes you need to be clever in how you present them.

ROTATE THOSE TOYS

Whatever Kitty's choice of playthings, just be sure you have plenty of them. And remember to rotate them, which means there should be at least two large batches of toys on hand at all times. Leave the first batch on the floor for two days while the second batch is stored in a closet. After two days, rotate them. Take the ones from the closet and place them on the floor, then take the ones from the floor and put them in the closet. Repeat this procedure every two days and you'll create a fresh and interesting environment for Kitty. Clever cat kitties, just like human kiddies, become bored with the same old toys. Without toy rotation it would be like playing Scrabble every day of the year. It might be fun at first but it gets to the point where enough is enough. If you take away those toys and then return them a few days later, they'll seem like brand-new playthings all over again. I kind of hate to admit it, but I guess you could say we're faking out our feline friends.

WHAT A SPORT! YOU GAVE KITTY
ONE SCRATCHING POST

Most cat owners supply their cats with one scratching post. Big deal. As I've explained before, I believe cats are very intelligent animals, more intelligent than many experts and some owners think they are. This intelligent creature is *bored to death* with only *one* scratching post. If those telltale pieces of furniture stuffing are still stuck to Kitty's paws or the carpet fringe is missing, then your cat is in the inquisitive, curious "I'm-too-bright-to-be-content-with-one-scratching-post" category. These cats need more, more, more.

MAKE YOUR OWN SCRATCHING POSTS

If you're independently wealthy, then by all means save yourself some trouble and go out and buy a bunch of scratching posts, poles, pads, and all the variations currently on the market. Rotate and change them frequently as I suggested you do with the toys. But if the thought of spending hundreds of dollars on scratching posts, poles and the like is not appealing to you, or if you've decided you simply won't get a second job to support Kitty's habit, take advantage of the freebies at the supermarket. Try using cardboard boxes and brown paper bags (never use plastic bags or any bag with handles—they're dangerous and could suffocate the cat). I think everyone on the planet knows that if you put a paper bag or box on the floor, Kitty will be sniffing and smelling and wandering in and out of it within minutes, if not seconds. It's something like Kitty's Big Adventure, because the items are brand-new to her environment and are full of interesting and exciting odors. Cats have a grand old time exploring what supermarkets give away at no charge. She'll think it's kitty heaven.

KITTY CONDOS

Don't be timid. Take the use of those cardboard boxes one step further—*build a kitty condo or duplex apartment.* Place together several strong cardboard boxes, cutting out a few holes in each so Kitty can climb in, out, and around her new co-op. Don't be afraid to be a little creative, particularly if you want to save money. Save your old carpet remnants or get friendly with the local carpet distributor or installer. Grab those odd-sized, leftover small pieces that get thrown out. Glue them to the sides of the boxes and *voilà!*—a cheap, instant scratching post. What's best about these do-it-yourself posts is, because they cost you nothing but five minutes of labor, you can change them all the time, keeping Kitty on her toes—literally.

If you're the reserved type and find it difficult to hustle the local merchants for scrap carpet remnants, it's still cheaper to buy some inexpensive doormats than it is to buy most scratching posts. Wait for a sale and buy a bunch.

BE CREATIVE

Don't fall into the old trap of using all the carpet with the nap side facing out. Many owners who swear their cats don't like scratching posts are amazed to learn their kitty simply prefers to scratch on rougher surfaces, including the underside of the carpet. Some cat owners know this already. They spend a lifetime smoothing out the ends of area rugs after Kitty has taken it upon herself to flip over the edges and scratch on the carpet's underside.

I once had a client who was not particularly wealthy and believed that the best investment she could make for her future were Persian and Oriental rugs. She purchased them whenever she could and thought of them as her savings account and retirement fund all rolled into one. She believed they would increase in value more than anything else her money could buy, or any yield from the bank. She kept the carpets properly stored in an unused bedroom in her home and rarely went in to check them. But one day she did and got the shock of her life. Upon her inspection she found that each and every one had been clawed and scratched on the underside. Her cat had reached the ends of each rolled carpet and had a ball clawing and kneading away to her heart's content. Fortunately, the damage was on the carpet backing, so while it had made the carpets less than perfect and therefore less valuable, nothing was visible from the carpet top so it wasn't a total loss. What could have been a terrible disaster had bearable negative results.

So experiment. Besides the traditional scratching paraphernalia, set up a taste test, or scratching preference test. Give Kitty the option of scratching something with the carpet nap exposed and something with the carpet backing facing outward. See what your little scratching expert prefers. In order to play it safe and keep the fuzzy little clawer interested, why not make up a few of each?

TRY A LOG

Try a what? Yup, a log or a piece of wood about the size used for a large wood-burning stove or fireplace. Some cats just love to do their stretching and scratching on wood so that no matter what you try, nothing else will do. After checking it first for bugs, bring the wood into the house and place it where Kitty likes to do her scratching. If she's a wood clawer she'll be delighted at the new addition to her inventory. What's best is if you can replace the piece every few days with another piece. If you don't have a wood source of your own, make a deal with someone you know who has a fireplace or wood-burning stove. Gung-ho owners can even bring larger pieces into the house. It's a thrill when you see Kitty's eyes light up. Yes, it is a bit of extra work but it may be the easiest step you can take to protect your belongings.

GET THAT CAT OUT OF THE HOUSE

Day in, day out, sitting in the house. Yuck! Kitty needs a reprieve. Get her out of the house. Take her on a few excursions. Give her something else to think about other than what piece of furniture she's going to attack today.

CORRECTIONS FOR CHEWING AND SCRATCHING

At the risk of repeating myself for the umpteenth time, I'm not fond of using corrections for changing behavior. I'd much rather concentrate on what's causing the problem and then make sure I'm meeting Kitty's needs. Once those steps are in place, the incorrect behavior almost always miraculously disappears. Cats don't want to be bad, but sometimes because of what the owner does or doesn't do they have no choice.

If you believe that you absolutely must use corrections, try the following:

Bad tasting and smelling no chew/no scratching products are available at pet counters everywhere. Different ones seem to be effective with different cats. Don't despair if after trying a few, Kitty still likes to scratch the sides of your chair or nibble the tassles of your decorative pillows. Experiment with a few more of the products and you'll probably find one Kitty dislikes. The only problem is that some of them smell so foul, they tend to keep away people, too.

Use balloons to keep Kitty from jumping on or scratching furniture. Blown-up balloons can be taped to the sides of chairs or walls, or anywhere Kitty is scratching. The balloons break when Kitty scratches or jumps, and even if you're not at home, our little leaping scratcher receives a correction, just as if some supreme being from above was in the house to tell her no. As an extra precaution, balloons should be sprayed with a no-chew product.

Important note: Balloons should never be used for a chewing problem and should only be used by owners who are 100 percent certain that Kitty would never consider chewing or swallowing them.

Aluminum foil is great if Kitty has staked out a few favorite spots for clawing. Place the foil around those special areas. Many cats are uncomfortable walking on it—the crinkly feeling underfoot seems too strange for them.

Or, you can fill some empty soda pop or beer cans with twenty pennies. Put tape over the opening and place the cans wherever Kitty is chewing, scratching, or jumping. Again, you don't have to be around for Kitty to find out that even though she's unsupervised, she can't get away with her mischievous deeds. If Kitty the thief jumps on the counter to steal food (or jumps on the furniture to eat or claw it) the cans fall down and make a startling noise—Kitty will get the point.

For really dedicated chewers, jumpers, and scratchers for

whom nothing seems to work, try one of the battery-operated door alarms. Some companies make alarms that can be slipped under the door so that when it opens the alarm is triggered. These alarms are a little hard to find, so try catalogs and shops specializing in products for travelers—the alarms are touted as being perfect for hotel room security. Place a few door alarms around Kitty's hot spots and when she steps on one, a shrill sound will send her on her way.

If Kitty has a penchant for eating your plants, try the techniques I've discussed above. You might also consider getting Kitty a plant of her own (sold at some pet shops and through certain catalogs). Some cats have a real physiological need to eat greens. Whether or not Kitty eats plants, be sure that none of the plants in your home are poisonous to pets. The list of offending plants is long, so check with your local plant nursery.

HOME SHOULD BE LIKE A KITTY HEALTH SPA
Kitty's play area should rival a Jack LaLanne workout area (see page 151). Her increased options will help eliminate bad behavior. She will be happier, which will make you happier, and your home will remain intact. Best of all, Kitty will get a lot more fun out of life.

DECLAWING—THE HOT DEBATE

Call me a naturalist or an old-fashioned guy but I don't like to tamper with Mother Nature just because it's more convenient for me. I guess that sums up my feelings about declawing. A supreme being much more knowledgeable than I decided Kitty should be born with nails. So until that being tells me to do something about removing those nails, I'll stand hard and fast in my position against declawing.

As far as I'm concerned no cat should be declawed. In particular, cats allowed outdoors should *never, ever* be declawed, no matter what the owner's rationalization might be. Outdoor cats need to protect themselves, and nature provided nails as a big part of their defense mechanism.

Most owners have cats declawed because they scratch and claw up their possessions. As you know by now, I'd much rather educate the clawing kitty as to what she may or may not scratch. It's really not as hard as you think. Remember: You can't teach a cat not to scratch but you can teach a cat *what* to scratch.

Fighting between cats in the same household is the second biggest incentive for owners to want to declaw their cats. But here's the rub! Although declawing will certainly eliminate the damage cats can do by scratching at each other, it does nothing about the much more serious damage that can be caused when one nasty cat bites another. These wounds often abscess badly. Cat owners shouldn't be lulled into the false sense of security that comes from removing the claws. If your cats are suffering due to a fighting household, it's best to get to the root of the problem and resolve it. (See chapter on First Kitty Psychology—How to Introduce a Second Pet to Your Cat— Avoiding Fights.)

Opinions differ on whether declawing is physically harmful to cats. Some say it's simply minor surgery. Others say X rays of the bone structure of Kitty's legs before and after declawing show a marked difference that's caused by his having to balance himself unnaturally. Without the nails, physical stress is placed on the legs, where it wasn't intended to be.

My favorite argument is when I'm told declawing doesn't hurt the cat. There's only one thing wrong with this statement—I've never heard a cat say it.

If you've already declawed your cat, don't feel guilty about it. It's over and done with and you thought you were doing the right thing. But for all future kitties in your life, think twice about it. In nature's grand plan, it's probably best if the human race keeps its hands off of God's creatures, particularly when there's no medical or humane benefit. Declawing is a quick fix to the destruction problem, but a better fix is to educate the cat. Besides, way too many indoor cats escape to the great outdoors at least once or twice in their lifetimes. Leaving them defenseless, without their nails, is simply out of the question.

TEACHING KITTY TO WALK
ON A LEASH

Here I go again. Of all the new and unusual ideas described in this book, the one that will make the biggest difference in the lives of cats is teaching them to walk on a leash. Unfortunately for me, I know the postman will be delivering bags of negative mail to my office because of this suggestion. Critics will have a grand time chopping me up. They'll say teaching cats to walk on leashes will threaten the dignity and independence of felines. That's okay—I'm prepared to take the heat. Anytime something innovative is suggested, there's bound to be a certain percentage of people who object. Some protest for what they believe to be legitimate reasons, while others raise their voices just for the heck of it. As a pioneer in several areas of the animal behavior world, I've met with great skepticism before. I've had the last laugh and have seen the difference some of my concepts made in the well-being of pets as they live in today's society.

In the early 1970s I was inundated with criticism when my work with pet-facilitated therapy, which teaches pets to assist the physically and mentally disabled, received media notoriety. Back then there weren't any fancy names like pet-facilitated therapy, there was just me putting two and two together. It didn't take a genius to figure out that the emotional bond between human and pet could help disabled people. I also don't think it was so special (and still don't) when I taught various animals to perform basic tasks for people with physical limitations. For years I had trained dogs to retrieve scent articles (small dumbbells and similar objects) for dog-show competitions. Teaching dogs to use the same responses to pick up items dropped by people confined to wheelchairs was no big deal. Using additional training methods, a pet could alert a deaf or hearing-impaired owner to a ringing doorbell, whistling tea kettle, or their crying baby. Cats play equally important roles in pet-facilitated therapy. Their small size and ability to use a litter box makes them perfect pet companion candidates when a larger dog with daily walking requirements isn't feasible for the very elderly or housebound.

Missy was one of those cats. She brought friendship and love into Elinore's life. Although Elinore was in her early nineties, she was witty and intelligent, but her old arthritic bones just wouldn't move the way they used to. Elinore was lucky enough to be able to continue to live in her own home, with nurses or housekeepers stopping in daily. But Elinore longed for a little special love. Her husband passed away years ago and her children had all moved far from home in pursuit of their careers and families. One of Elinore's neighbors contacted me after hearing what wonderful effects pets could have on the elderly. We matched up Elinore with an older cat, one that was well past its kitten shenanigans stage. Arrangements were made with the neighbor that if anything should happen to Elinore she would continue caring for Missy. With all the details in place, Missy came to live with Elinore—and what a life they had! Elinore talked to Missy and Missy talked to Elinore—they became fast friends. They ate their meals, napped in the sun, and loved to watch all the Hollywood gossip TV programs together. And as if fate had a master plan they died within days of each other, both from natural causes. Missy and Elinore were a grand combination and brought love and joy into each other's lives.

How was I to know that only a few dozen people in the entire world were working on things like this? I did it because it just made sense. I also thought everyone else was doing it. Well, they weren't. As strange as it may sound now that pet-facilitated therapy is widely accepted, back then I had to fight every step of the way. Achieving the same status for hearing ear dogs that Seeing Eye dogs had was a major accomplishment in itself. In retrospect it sounds absurd, but years ago I actually had to aid in the fight to get laws passed allowing hearing ear dogs to accompany their owners wherever it was necessary, including places where pets were prohibited.

Bear with me for one more example. Of all the controversial things with which I've been involved, the opposition I faced on this case best illustrates why I decided, regardless of the critics, to stick to my guns about teaching cats to walk on a leash. This story is about Mark, who was a young boy at the time. To my dying day I'll never forget him. Mark has Down's Syndrome. As is often the case with children having disabilities, he was shunned by the neighborhood kids, and so it was easy for him to withdraw into an isolated home life. I was called in to help Mark work with Buffy, his new, shaggy, golden-tan dog. I was to show Mark what to do with Buffy and then it was up to Mark to practice with his pet pal every day. And did Mark practice! He was faithful to his lessons with "The Buff." Grooming Buffy was part of Mark's responsibilities, too. There was never a hair out of place.

More than anything else, Mark wanted Buffy to learn to play dead when shot and to take a bow after performing his repertoire of responses. I showed Mark what to do, Mark showed Buffy what to do, and in no time the two of them were showing off to the neighborhood locals. Everyone stopped to say hello to the twosome. Mark and Buffy became fast friends, providing each other with warmth, love, and a very special companionship. It was a special highpoint in my life.

So, imagine my surprise when a lot of negative comments came my way because of this early work with pets and the disabled. *New York Newsday,* a prestigious newspaper, printed an article about my little friend with Down's Syndrome and how the dog helped to change his life. At the end of the article there was a quote from a well-respected doctor associated with a national child health and development institute. He questioned the emotional support a pet can provide, asking how you measure a pet's emotional capability and how it can be transmitted. The end quote was that he thought the whole thing was based on a tenuous assumption. Well, I—and a lot of other animal professionals—proved these naysayers wrong. Now, pet-facilitated therapy is a recognized medical phenomenon. Higher learning institutions all over the world extol its virtues.

Yes, I have been called a pioneer in the field of pet-facilitated therapy. Yes, I was one of the first people in the world who taught pets to hear for the deaf. Yes, I was one of the earliest advocates of hugging and kissing healthy pets when critics claimed we'd all die from their germs. I've been challenged before and stuck it out and I'll probably be challenged again.

I get a real kick out of watching animals, seeing the love they dole out with no strings attached and how they make me and everyone else smile, no matter how tough the day. So when I see something that's wrong or something that makes sense I just have to get involved. In Kitty's case, a behavior must be changed. The human animal has taken away the cat's freedom by either forcing her to live indoors or by running the risk of being splattered on the street. I just have to act on something like this.

ARE YOU READY?
So, here we go, this is the statement that will set off a thousand typewriters—or at least a few hundred word processors. I'm ready for the mail but, before you write, please just hear me out.

All cats should be taught to walk on a leash and harness. Please note that I said *all* cats, not most cats or a few cats or cats with special life-styles, but *all* cats. Let's start by discussing why.

WHY ALL CATS SHOULD BE TAUGHT
TO WALK ON A LEASH

First, there's the obvious reason. Leashes give owners a secure means of control when kitties need to be moved from one environment to the next, such as when it's time to go to the vet. Unless a cat has been properly adjusted to a cat carrier (which is not always the case with the general cat-owning population), it means dragging out the carrier and then playing hide-and-seek with Kitty. The frightened furball probably took one look at the carrier, knew what was about to take place, and split. Once you've dragged the now Jekyll/Hyde kitty out from under the bed or other hiding area (hopefully without your suffering any major wounds), then comes the dreaded moment when Kitty gets stuffed in the box. Mind you, I'm not advocating stuffing the little terror into the box, but that's what generally happens with anxious cats and their owners. By this point, many cats have spread each of their four tiny, but amazingly steellike legs in four totally different directions, making their approach into the box sort of like fitting fifteen college students into one telephone booth. Okay, okay, *whew!* now you've accomplished this part. The cat is securely in the box, but there's so much upset taking place you know this can't be the right thing. One of a couple of scenarios could happen next. Kitty is either screaming and yowling, or she's curled up in the corner, hugging the back of the carrier so tightly she might as well be wallpapered to the container. Of course, both scenarios are accompanied by shaking and other appropriate nervous reactions—uncontrollable tail twitching, heavy panting, and, in some cases, spontaneous urination or bowel movements all over herself. Is this good? I think not. Score one point for teaching Kitty to walk on a leash and to be happy with her newfound freedom.

Another very important reason for teaching a cat to walk on a leash is plain old boredom. I've said this before, but it's important enough to say again—cats are too intelligent to be

expected to live in the same home, surrounded by the same
four walls, watching the same soap operas, day in and day out,
365 days a year, for the next ten to twenty years of their lives.
As far as I'm concerned, this is a jail sentence of cruel and
unusual punishment. Even prison inmates are allowed outdoors
for fresh air and exercise.

Teaching Kitty to walk on a leash will allow her so many
extra freedoms. She'll be able to experience the joys of the
world and become a better companion to her owner. After all
she *wants* to go with you. She doesn't want to be alone all day,
never visiting Grandma or seeing the cousins. Kitty wants to
know why she can't go on a Sunday drive with the rest of the
family or on a quick trip to the hardware store. If Kitty were a
dog I bet she'd get some of these luxuries. Let's not make cats
third-class citizens. They deserve much more. Score a second
point for teaching Kitty to walk on a leash.

Fear of escape has a lot to do with preventing us from taking
Kitty on special outings. The fear of a frightened, unrestrained
cat jumping from your arms and running off, never to be found
again, is a real one. Carrying an unrestrained cat to a strange
environment is an irresponsible act. Just as I caution dog owners that even the best trained dog should never be off his leash,
I give the same advice to cat owners. But when taught to walk
on a leash, Kitty can journey safely beyond her four walls.
She'll be out and about so frequently that she won't associate
every trip outside with a negative experience. Kitty will become desensitized to being out of her environment. It will
become a casual happening, rather than the main wrestling
event. Everyone is happier. Score the third point for teaching
a cat to walk on a leash.

And then there are the times when owners really need to
travel with their cats. Take Fred for example. I met Fred and
his actor/owner on a flight from New York to Los Angeles. In
order to control an illness Fred required several daily injections

and his owner really didn't trust anyone else to dispense that type of care to his cat buddy. So the actor and his pal traveled the country together. But was Fred cooped up in a cat carrier during all these travel days? No way. Fred was leash trained and on our flight enjoyed the luxury of sitting on his owner's lap. And was Fred a hit with the passengers and airline attendants! His loving and social manner made the flight seem shorter for everyone.

Contrary to what you may be thinking right now, it's not all that difficult to teach Kitty to walk on a leash. I know you may feel that cats are not meant to do this, but did nature intend for cats to stay indoors all their lives or to be hit by cars on busy streets? Modern society dictates that we all have to adapt—cats too.

STEP-BY-STEP INSTRUCTIONS FOR STEPPING OUT WITH KITTY

STEP 1: PURCHASING THE RIGHT OUTFIT

In Kitty's case, this is a properly fitting harness or collar. Harnesses are preferable for a number of reasons. They provide a secure fit, preventing Kitty from wriggling out. They also eliminate stress to the neck should she become frightened and try to pull away. The downside to a harness is the annoyance of getting it onto her. Some kitties decide that under no circumstances will they sit still while you maneuver a harness on them. Before jumping to the conclusion that Kitty hates the harness, be sure to follow the steps on how to adjust a cat to one (see page 129). Most cats, if given the opportunity, will become comfortable with a harness.

For cats and owners who simply prefer collars I have no real objections, providing the cat is not a "puller" type, and neck or throat injuries are not a legitimate threat. Also, owners must be absolutely certain the fit is secure. Collars must be sufficiently tight to prevent them from slipping over Kitty's head, even if she becomes frightened and tries to bolt away. To check the fit of the collar, tighten it to the point where you're unable to pull it up over Kitty's ears even if she were trying to wriggle free. Be sure there's a drop of space between the collar and Kitty's neck to ensure that the collar is not too tight, that it doesn't interfere with her breathing or comfort. Be a thorough inspector. Carelessness can cause a loose cat.

Don't use one of the elasticized collars designed to break or stretch if the cat is caught on something. A pop-away or stretch collar should be used only as an everyday collar (heaven forbid Kitty gets caught on something, she would be able to escape). They're not designed for walking purposes.

Leashes are easier to work with. They are available at pet counters everywhere (leashes made for very small dogs will also do well). A good cat leash should be made from an extremely light material. Leather, nylon, or cotton are all suitable provided there is very little weight to the leash. Strength is not nearly as important as it would be for a powerful sixty-pound dog, but the leash still shouldn't be flimsy. Be a good consumer and check the construction, particularly around the handle and clip area. Is it stitched well? Are these areas reinforced with extra stitching or with grommets? Check for loose strings. Often the lesser quality items are not finished well (telltale thread ends are the biggest tipoff). Don't be afraid to pull, pick, or use your fingernails to check a product. I'm not suggesting you ruin the shopkeeper's merchandise, but if you notice within a few seconds of your product testing that the leash seems worse for the wear and tear, then I guarantee that Kitty will have it looking like a disaster in no time. Worse, it may not be safe, and may break apart when you least expect it.

Next, take a good hard look at the clip—that's the area

attaching the leash to the harness or collar. If there's one area where many cat product manufacturers could really clean up their acts, this is it. Too many cat leashes have fasteners that are just slightly better than cheap key rings. I even hesitate to call them clips—in my opinion, they're glorified junk. Leash fasteners should be a standard clip you would most commonly see on a good dog leash. Quality cat leashes use the same type of clip, just a smaller version. Be sure the weight of the clip is not too heavy and that it's adequate to provide the necessary safety.

Play around with the clip's snap mechanism. It should open and close properly, not too easily yet not with too much difficulty. And it should close tightly. After you test a few different clips on several varieties of leashes you'll see what I mean about the difference. It's obvious once you know what you're looking for.

STEP 2: GETTING KITTY COMFY

Now here's the part you've been worried about. Just how do you get that cat of yours adjusted to a leash, harness, or collar? Be patient and make sure all the practice steps take place indoors for now. When you're beginning, it's tough to compete with what's going on outdoors.

WHOA! WHAT IS THIS STUFF?

Let's start with the assumption that Kitty has never before seen any of this walking paraphernalia. Place Kitty's wardrobe items in one of her favorite lounging areas (be sure she can't get tangled up in it) and leave them there for a week or so. Allow her to become familiar with them, sniffing and pawing until she realizes they're not threatening. Once this is accomplished, gently lay the harness or collar on her back or neck (don't actually put it on) for a second or two several times a day until you notice that she seems to tolerate it well. Next, place the harness or collar on Kitty for a few minutes each day. Let her walk around the house with it on. Most cats will act a bit strange at first but will begin to take it in stride very quickly. Each time the harness or collar is on the cat be sure you do something special, like scratching the little furball in her favorite spot or feeding her a favorite treat (but in moderation—I'd much rather give her hugging and loving than food rewards). Let Kitty think that every time she sees the harness or the walking collar something wonderful is going to happen. If every experience is really special, she'll actually start to look forward to it. Don't get sloppy. Every time the harness or collar is placed on the cat during the training process, be sure she thinks there's going to be a party just for her! We all learn through association—and cats are no different. Let this association be the most positive thing she's ever experienced.

As Kitty adjusts, gradually extend the time she wears the harness or collar. Be sure you're there to supervise, just in case she gets caught on something.

STEP 3: USING THE REAL THING

Okay, so now Kitty's enjoying the harness or collar so much, she actually goes over and nudges it. Well, then it's certainly time to progress to the leash. To begin, attach the leash to the harness or collar for just a minute or two. Use the same type of positive reinforcement you used when acclimating the cat to the harness or collar. Don't try to walk Kitty. Simply attach the leash and let the furball do what she wants, which may very possibly be nothing but sitting there feeling and looking awkward. Practice for a few minutes each day. Allow Kitty to walk where she pleases, dragging the leash behind her. Continue for a week or so until she is moseying around the house with the leash attached. Increase to longer periods of time but, again, be sure to supervise her in case she gets caught on anything.

STEP 4: LET KITTY DECIDE WHERE YOU'RE GOING

Once Kitty's comfortable with the leash it's time to start walking together. Or, should I say, start walking where *he* wants to. Pick up the end of the leash and actually follow him around. Don't try to get him to walk in the direction you want. Just follow. Practice this for a few days. When he looks comfortable, you're ready to teach the little student to walk with you.

FIGHT OFF THE
CATS-CAN'T-BE-TRAINED MENTALITY

For anyone thinking leash training sounds complicated, think again. This procedure is no different than recommended procedures for puppies. Many dogs start off with a complete dislike for the leash and collar and their education amounts to something like taming a bucking bronco. I'm sure you've seen dogs reacting and overreacting to some of their first experiences on leashes. Well, as I've said time and time again, cats are no different. Just use good, solid teaching techniques—be patient, kind, and take it a little at a time. It's not very much work, just a few minutes each day. Anyone who can leash train a dog can leash train a cat. It's that simple. Cats are certainly smart enough to learn how to walk on a leash. Anyone thinking differently is insulting the felines of the world.

STEP 5: GOING WHERE YOU WANT TO GO

Once little Kitty gets the idea of walking and stalking around the house while you sheepishly follow behind, it's time to teach her to go where *you* want to go. While giving Kitty so much verbal encouragement that the neighbors think it's time to commit you to the local asylum, begin walking in the direction of your choice. Your voice should be sweet, high pitched (men will need to practice this), and exciting. Kitty will probably take a few steps in your direction, then her mental alarm will ring. She'll realize this is where *you* want her to go—and that's not quite what she has in mind. Any self-respecting cat, or dog for that matter, will immediately put on the brakes, firmly placing all four paws on the ground and giving you a look that translates to "Go ahead, just *try* to move me." She'll then dig in for the battle of the wills. When this happens, don't get suckered into playing it her way. Don't think that because the little darling's stopped dead in her tracks you need to drag and pull her. I'm quite sure all cats have read advanced scientific material and are adept at applying basic physics—the more an owner pulls in one direction the more the cat resists and pulls in the other.

MY SECRET WEAPON FOR CATS WHO WON'T BUDGE AN INCH

When Kitty's glued to the floor and refuses to move, a special technique needs to be employed, called little tug and release. With the least amount of effort, give the leash the lightest possible tug and then quickly and immediately release the tug so that the leash hangs loosely. If Kitty doesn't move, repeat this procedure several times in a row, taking a four- or five-second pause between each tug. While you're doing this, continue with excited high-pitched verbal encouragement.

Don't be afraid to get down on your hands and knees to encourage Kitty from her eye level. Don't be disillusioned if your little furball only moves six inches or so on the first dozen attempts. Keep at it, as any good teacher would, and you'll start to notice little breakthroughs. One day she'll just get up and walk around the house with you. You'll celebrate, pat yourself on the back, and call the relatives at work and let them know what a genius cat you have. Then, of course, the next day Kitty will look at you with that old give-me-a-break, I-know-you-can't-be-serious look. When this happens, don't despair. It's 100 percent normal for intelligent animals; they'll test the limits to see what they can get away with. Just keep plugging away with the little tug and release technique.

DON'T MISUSE THIS TECHNIQUE

Let's review the important points of the little tug and release method once again, because applying this technique incorrectly may actually discourage Kitty from walking. The tug should be ever so gentle, not a pull and not a drag, but the slightest little tug that must be followed by an immediate release. There should be no tension on the collar or harness. Wait several seconds between each little tug and release. As you work on this procedure it helps to actually say to yourself "tug-release, tug-release, tug-release." For whatever reason, probably dating back to the old drag-the-dog-if-he-doesn't-want-to-walk approach that so many early training books advocated, owners forget to release after the tug. That's exactly what we don't want. We're not looking to place constant pressure on the cat, but just to give the *gentlest little nudge* in the right direction. Practice every day for a few minutes. It's not necessary, and it's not even a good idea, to have a lengthy once-a-day training session while Kitty is learning to walk on a leash. It's much better suited for the cat, and more than likely to fit into your busy schedule, to practice a few minutes here and there. Keep up the praise; it's easy to forget, particularly if Kitty is a little slow to walk. The more frustrated you become, the less praise you'll probably use—the direct opposite of what should be done. Reluctant cats need all the praise and confidence building they can get.

If frustration strikes, don't take it out on the cat. Go beat up on your pillow, then make yourself a cup of coffee or tea, or maybe even pour a glass of wine. Then take a much needed break and try it again.

IT'S DARKEST JUST BEFORE THE DAWN

One last thought of encouragement for owners who are really having trouble achieving good results: Cats have an uncanny way of responding and getting things right just when things look the bleakest. Just when you think Kitty is never going to get the hang of it, out of nowhere she'll pick herself up and start walking all over the place like an Olympic athlete. Kitty always knew what you were doing; she was just having a good time watching you sweat it out.

STEP 6: TRANSFERRING KITTY'S EDUCATION TO THE GREAT OUTDOORS

Now it's time to tackle the great outdoors. If Kitty's never been outside, you'll have to take it a bit slow. There's a big, frightening world out there, full of all sorts of strange sights, smells, and noises. If Kitty is the skittish type then it will help to first desensitize her to outside noise by softly playing a tape recording or sound effects record of trucks, sirens, traffic, etc. Gradually increase the volume over a period of weeks as Kitty seems relaxed with the current level of sound. Before expecting your cat to go for a long walk around the neighborhood, be sure she feels comfortable outside. Sometimes the best plan of action is to do nothing, meaning that you simply go outside with Kitty on a leash and sit on the stoop. Just let Kitty see and hear the world go by. This is particularly important for city cats or for cats who live in high traffic areas. You'll know when the cat has adapted to its new environment. She'll develop a certain relaxed look. Nervous tail twitching will stop and she will become curious about the new sights, possibly even wandering off a little to explore. When this occurs, it's time to take her for the smallest of walks, just as you did during the first steps during indoor leash training. Let Kitty take you where she wants to go. Follow her until she gets the idea of walking outdoors on a leash. After a week or so, encourage her to walk where you want to go. Lots of encouragement and praise is needed here—so don't be surprised when passersby throw you some pretty strange glances. Don't let it get to you. You're doing the kindest thing you can for today's cat—you're setting her free.

STEP 7: DON'T BE FRUSTRATED IF YOU OR YOUR KITTY STUDENT GETS LEFT BACK

If you find that you're having trouble with any of the previous steps, don't get frustrated. It simply means you've advanced a little too quickly. Go back to the steps preceding the problem and spend a little more time perfecting the weak areas.

IT'S GRATIFYING TO KNOW I'VE MADE A DIFFERENCE

As strange as my suggestions for teaching your cat to walk on a leash may sound to you today, think of what they sounded like years ago when I first insisted cats had to get out of the house. One of my most rewarding experiences took place back then. I was appearing on a weekly television program, *Saturday Morning,* in New York, hosted by the wonderful television legend Gene Rayburn. On the program I demonstrated that cats could and should walk on a leash. A few weeks after that particular show I was on the New York State Thruway traveling to my farm in upstate New York. I pulled into a rest stop to buy some lunch and there was a cat on a leash stretching his legs along with his owner. In a flash the owner recognized me and came running over. "Warren, Warren, aren't you Warren Eckstein, from television?" she said. Sheepishly I admitted I was. Thrilled to see me, the woman proudly showed off her cat, who was walking everywhere on a leash, enjoying his break from the car. "If it wasn't for you," she said, "Sylvester wouldn't be with me. I never would have taken him on a vacation with the family. He would have been forced to stay in the kennel, which he hates. He always comes back so sick and thin. But just look at him—look how happy he is to be with us! We're all going on vacation together, isn't it great?''

Yes, it was. I got back into my car feeling quite overwhelmed. When you're on a lot of television and radio programs you know you're reaching many people, but when you actually see the results of your efforts it's a very special experience. I was thrilled.

So go to it. Give your little Sylvester the opportunity to · enjoy life. Once the training process is over, that little ball of fur will thank you a thousand times.

TEACHING KITTY TO COME
WHEN CALLED

Dogs come when they're called. So of course Kitty can be taught the same thing. Cats are bright enough to learn most basic instructions. It just takes practice, perseverance, and an ounce of know-how. Because a cat who comes when called is a foreign concept to many owners (most everyone has been indoctrinated into thinking cats can't be taught to come on command), I've put together ten easy steps for teaching our favorite furballs this very important response.

WARREN ECKSTEIN'S 10 EASY STEPS TO TEACHING
KITTY TO COME WHEN CALLED

1. Use Kitty's name to help grab her attention. "Kitty, come."
2. Use Kitty's name only for positive things.
3. Never call Kitty for something unpleasant or negative. If you're going to give her medicine, you should go to her.
4. During the initial training, it will help if you practice from

floor level so Kitty can make better eye contact with you.

5. EACH AND EVERY TIME Kitty comes to you, praise her to the hilt. Don't be lazy about the positive reinforcement.

6. Only use the come command when you're in a position to follow it through if Kitty doesn't come. There's nothing worse than letting Kitty know she can pick and choose when she wants to listen to you.

7. Talk to the other members of the family. Be sure they're not running around all day long calling her and then ignoring her if she doesn't respond (or worse, if she does). Nothing will ruin your chances of success more than inconsistency within the family.

8. Don't have Kitty participate in ten minutes of practice lessons in which all you do is repeat the same thing. It's boring and bound to turn her off.

9. Instead, call her once or twice half a dozen times during the day. Practice a little bit here and there.

10. If Kitty doesn't come right away and you've spent way too much time cajoling her into the response, be sure to praise her when she finally decides to mosey on over. You may find this awfully hard to do after you've been coaxing the fuzzy darling for fifteen minutes, but it's the end response she'll remember. Don't blow it by not pouring on the praise. Bang on your pillow afterward if you must, but don't take it out on Kitty.

STEP 5 CAN MAKE ALL THE
DIFFERENCE IN THE WORLD

All ten steps are important. Ignore any one of them and you'll reduce your chance of success by 10 percent. Ignore several of them and the risk factor for noncompliance shoots up proportionately. However, if I had to narrow in on any one step that can really make the big difference, it's step 5. *Each and every time she comes to you, don't get lazy. Praise her to the hilt.*

If Kitty believes that each time she comes to you fabulous things will happen, just watch how quickly she bounds right over. That's the deal you have to make with yourself and with her. You must stop whatever you're doing and fuss over her like nothing she's ever seen before. Praise her like crazy and, if she's friendly enough, kiss and hug her and give her a little kitty massage. Try some scratching behind the ears. Every now and then give Kitty a little piece of her all-time favorite food. (Not too often, though. We don't want Kitty to become dependent on a food reward for her response. That's how you turn into one of those nutty people who have to run around the neighborhood shaking a box of cat food in order to get Kitty back in the house.) Let her think she just won the 50 million dollar lottery. Get the idea? Go overboard. Fuss, fuss, fuss all over her. When you're finished and you think you've done enough, just think of my nagging voice saying, "That's not enough. Do more, more, more."

Go to these extremes, and of course Kitty will want to come to you. Why shouldn't she? You're the most interesting and best deal in town. One quick word of caution—no matter how quickly Kitty responds to come when called, never allow her off leash when she's outdoors. It only takes one time of her not hearing you to be run down by a car or truck.

TEACHING KITTY TO SIT

Teaching Kitty to sit may or may not be on your priority list. Clearly, sitting on command is important for large dogs who gallop all over the house and terrorize guests but Kitty isn't Marmaduke or Howard Huge and teaching sit often takes a backseat to almost everything else.

Whether you want Kitty to sit when asked because it has some relevance to your life-style or if you've simply decided that Kitty needs to be mentally challenged, here are some simple steps for sit instruction.

THE GREAT ESCAPE

For better control during the lesson be sure Kitty's wearing a collar or harness. If you don't have some method to hang on to Kitty I guarantee she'll use remarkable talent and demonstrate her best disappearing act to escape from the clutches of any human being who even *thinks* of teaching her to sit on command.

HERE'S THE ROUTINE

1. Kneel alongside Kitty, facing her.
2. Using the hand closest to her neck place one or two fingers under her collar or harness.
3. Place the other hand under her rear end just above what would be called the knee joint if it were on the human body. If Kitty's nervous about being touched, see the chapter on massage (Chapter 6) for desensitizing her to being hand led.
4. Do the next two things at the exact same time: Using the hand that is holding on to the collar—*very gently* and *ever so slightly* lift upwards, then backwards—*easing* her body weight towards her rear end. The instructions "very gently" and "slight lift" mean just that—the slightest little teeny weeny bit of pressure just to show Kitty in which direction she should be moving her body parts.
5. Using the hand which is below the tush—*very gently* push and tuck in Kitty's derriere.
6. Say "Sit" with an emphasis on the *t* in sit. This will help Kitty distinguish the "sit" word from other words in her vocabulary. Don't use her name in conjunction with sit—it may excite Kitty and cause her to pop up rather than sit down. This advice differs greatly from commands indicat-

ing motion, such as come when called or walking on a leash where Kitty's name should be used to encourage her movement.
7. During the entire process speak gently and soothingly to the little student.

EXPECT KITTY TO SAY "NO WAY"

It's only normal for Kitty to decide she's not going to have a darn thing to do with this sitting on command nonsense. No matter how bad things are going, be patient and *make it fun.* Act like a drill sergeant and she'll fight you all the way. Treat sit like a new party game and things will fall into place much faster. Tell Kitty she's wonderful. Pat her on the head and scratch her behind the ears. And as always, if Kitty's friendly, smooch it up a little. You know my techniques by now—plenty of praise and love.

Results may not be quick in coming. This has a lot more to do with owner inexperience in working with a cat than it has to do with the cat's ability to learn. Don't give up. It will work out in the end and it may even take a few hundred tries. Remember, before learning sit many dog students take a few hundred tries of their own. Some canine owners actually need to seek out private lessons just to teach fidgety Fido to sit. Keep plugging away. You'll both get the hang of it with a little more practice.

TEACHING KITTY TO STAY

Is "stay" a command you associate exclusively with dogs? Well, Rover isn't the only housepet who can learn this handy response. Kitty certainly has the ability to understand and respond to the word "stay"—and he should learn it. There will be times when you'll be very happy that your little furball understands this basic communication.

FIRST, THE PRACTICAL APPLICATIONS

1. Kitty's at the vet and a bit anxious, not sure if he should tolerate the experience or try to make a fast break for the door. Hearing the word *stay* may just be that little extra reminder that's needed for him to remain exactly where he is. It will also help boost Kitty's confidence level when there's a verbal request from his beloved owner—one that he's heard hundreds of times before with no ill effects.

2. Guests are at the door. Kitty's waiting in the wings. She's tired of living out her life in the house. The furball is lacing up her sneakers, waiting for the big opportunity. The door opens and Kitty revs up her engine, getting ready to zoom past the door and into the great outdoors. The door cracks open and then it happens—that one dreaded word, *stay*. Kitty knows you're on to her. What's more, you've specifically instructed her to remain in place. The game's over.

3. Kitty's out and about or up and around. You need to get him but he's playing a one-sided game of hide and seek. You get close and Kitty takes off. There's that word again, *stay*. It solves a lot of problems.

4. Kitty needs help. She's caught her leg in something. Maybe there's some string wrapped around her neck or even a thumbtack in her paw. The more she fights against the pain, the more she hurts herself. *Stay*. She's come to trust that word. Kitty can focus on something she's being told and you can provide the desperately needed help. You just can't beat a little basic communication and understanding.

5. Kitty's got something in his eye and is pawing frantically at it. *Stay*. Now you can get it out for him.

6. Kitty's nails are too long and because Kitty struggles wildly your vet always seems to make them bleed. Make toenail clipping a do-it-yourself home project. Ear cleaning, too. *Stay* makes things a whole lot easier. The professional wres-

tling matchup between you and Hulk Kitty simply fails to materialize.

STAY IS EASY TO TEACH

I'd like to reiterate that cats can learn many responses. There's no big miracle behind teaching Kitty to stay. The only problem is that owners really don't believe it can be taught to her, so they project a self-defeating attitude in their approach—that's if they even attempt it at all.

If you're unsure Kitty will eventually respond, she'll pick up on your lack of confidence in no time. As I've said, cats are quite adept at reading the body language of humans. If Kitty knows that *you* know she'll never stay on command, surprise, surprise—nothing happens!

Keep in mind that all those wonderfully trained dogs didn't learn to "stay" overnight. Weeks or months of practice and reinforcement went into making them well-behaved. You know the old saying—practice makes perfect. There are no overnight successes here.

NOW, TO BEGIN

It's best to have a means of control when you start, preferably a leash or harness. You'll need a way to convince Kitty that the *stay* lesson doesn't mean *adiós, amigo*. You don't want him to take one look at you and decide he's out of there.

With Kitty in front of you, slip one or two fingers under his harness or collar, or place your hand on the leash close to where it attaches to the harness or collar. If you wish (and I do suggest it), give Kitty the hand signal for stay at the same time you tell him to stay. "Oh, sure," you're saying. "Now Warren's telling me Kitty's going to learn hand signals?" Well, why not? Do you really think Kitty doesn't have the innate intelligence to learn a few basic hand signals? In the wild, cats learn the meaning of many physical body signals. They have to in order to survive. While living in our domestic homes Kitty can certainly learn the hand signal for stay.

So back to the hand signal. The palm of your hand should face Kitty with the fingers pointing toward the floor. At the same time you give the hand signal, give him the command, *stay*. Don't use Kitty's name—we don't want him to first get excited by hearing it and then have to tell him to stay put. Only use Kitty's name for commands when you want him to move, like when you use *come*.

A LITTLE TRICK

When you're working on teaching Kitty to stay, it helps to draw out the word and spell it mentally as you say it. *S-t-a-y.* During the initial teaching stages drag it out for as long as the air in your lungs will last. Stay means Kitty should remain in one place for a while. By lengthening the word, you're cuing her to something that is supposed to be going on for more time than usual. If there also happens to be a dog in the house, feel free to use the same trick for Rover. It will work for him, too.

REPEAT, REPEAT, REPEAT YOURSELF

When you're practicing with Kitty, give the command constantly. Use the same type of repetition you experienced when learning the alphabet or multiplication tables. None of us were one-shot superstars when it came to learning the fundamentals of our education. Well, I wasn't, anyway.

HEY, KITTY,
NOW YOU'RE GETTING THE IDEA

When Kitty looks as if she's getting the point, slowly remove your hand that's been holding onto the collar, harness, or leash. Do it slowly, gradually easing off on the pressure. Kitty will sense you're giving her some slack and if she's a red-blooded, normal, healthy kitty she's going to seize the moment and fly right out of there. Wean her off the control that your hand was supplying. Please repeat, repeat, repeat *s-t-a-y*, *s-t-a-y*, *s-t-a-y*. And don't forget the praise!

KITTY GOES FOR HER PH.D.

After Kitty has the idea down pat, make things interesting. A little cautionary note, however. Don't move on to this until Kitty's picture-perfect in her stay response. Any weakness in the fundamentals will show up as a major fault in more advanced work. Tell her to stay and practice tossing things past her. Enlist family members to walk, then run by. I know that going to graduate school isn't everyone's cup of tea and you may not think a good response to "stay" is critical to your life with Kitty. I hate to break the news to you but you're wrong. Just review the six practical applications (and there are plenty more) at the beginning of the chapter. Stay certainly has its merits.

KEEPING KITTY FROM
RUNNING OUT THE DOOR

If I had a dollar for every indoor cat who bolted out the door, never to be seen again, I'd be a very rich man. Well, I'd rather not be wealthy and instead know that Kitty's snoozing safe and sound at home, comfy in her own bed.

When Kitty gets a certain mischievous glint in her eyes, *watch out*—you know she's packed her bags, put on a jogging suit, and is planning a little outdoor excursion. But Kitty may also be the slinking type of feline. These are the type of cats you never see approach the door. Rather, they sneak up a little at a time, ever so nonchalantly, and when the unsuspecting owner opens the door, *wham!* they're gone.

Pepe was one of these. His preferred approach was to wait until no one was watching, then the moment the door was open he'd speed past it like a jackrabbit. There was just one hitch: Pepe didn't go anywhere. He didn't want to go anywhere because he knew that in just a few minutes Mom and Dad would be outside with a handful of goodies as an enticement for him to come home. This very clever cat would sit just outside his owners' reach and whenever anyone made a grab for him, he simply moved a little to the left or a little to the right. Each time Pepe moved, the owners tossed him a goodie, hoping he wouldn't run any farther. And that's the way it went until Pepe was certain each and every goodie was gone. Then Pepe would pick up his fuzzy body, trot over to the door, meow for Mom and Dad to open it, sashay into the bedroom, lick and clean himself, and finally take a nap. It was Pepe's game and he had written the directions for how to play it.

That's how Mowdy was in the beginning. It was hard for him to adjust to a more confined life-style. He tried to get out all the time but when he managed one of his great escapes, like Pepe, he really didn't want to go anywhere. Mowdy was just interested in seeing to what extremes his pop would go to get him back. Well, we don't play those games in my house. Clearly, it was time for Mowdy to learn never to run out the door.

Respecting imaginary boundaries around the doors of a house or an apartment is one of the things every fearless feline should learn. It's easy to do and there are even two ways you can go about it.

USE WHAT KITTY ALREADY KNOWS

If you opted to teach Kitty the stay command, here's the perfect place to put it into practical application. It's not necessary to have fine-tuned the stay response so that Kitty remains in one position like a concrete statue, but it is necessary for him to have a general idea of the meaning of the command.

Pick a spot around the door that will give Kitty some sort of visual cue as to how far he may venture without your official okay for him to cross over the imaginary line. Depending on the layout of your home, it could be where the carpet stops and the tile around the door begins. It may be where the oak coat-rack or the umbrella stand is positioned. Practice placing Kitty at the correct side of the line of demarcation and telling him to stay. When he tries to move and walk past the boundary, tell him no. Repeat the process. Praise him for the right response. There's no magic involved here, it's simply a matter of practice and reinforcement. Do it often enough and Kitty will honor "the line."

USE PSYCHOLOGICAL REMINDERS

If you really don't have it in you to teach Kitty to stay, you can still accomplish good results in keeping Kitty from running out the door. Refer back to the section on scratching and clawing (page 108) and apply the soda-pop can, aluminum foil, balloon, or door alarm technique (whichever works best for your little whippersnapper). Line the imaginary cutoff point with one of these teaching aids. This strange decorating scheme will have to grace your home for a few weeks until Kitty gets the drift of staying away from that area. (You may want to postpone those dinner parties unless you enjoy being teased like heck by friends.)

Remove the equipment a little at a time, a few pieces every week or so, until everything's been taken away.

PRAISE, LOVE, HUG, KISS, AND
SCRATCH BEHIND THE EARS

Okay, okay so you're sick of hearing this by now. It's just that the importance of reinforcing good behavior cannot be empha-sized enough. Spend most of your time telling Kitty how well he's doing, and don't dwell on his mistakes. Praise him and do more loving, hugging, kissing, and scratching behind the ears than you ever thought was possible. With this type of positive attention, Kitty will live up to your expectations.

KITTY'S MEMORY LAPSE

When you get to the point at which all the training reminders have been removed, be prepared for Kitty to fake temporary amnesia and pretend she's forgotten everything just taught to her. It's normal for Kitty to test her limits. All you need to do is repeat the process. Yes, you may have to backtrack over your steps a few more times after that as well. Sometimes it helps to leave one of the teaching reminders in place long after you've completed the rest of the procedure. This will help jar Kitty's memory as to what she isn't allowed to do.

OY VAY, THIS IS SO MUCH WORK!

Is this all a lot of work? You bet it is! Will it help safeguard Kitty's well-being, keeping her from escaping and being lost forever or killed by street traffic? You bet it will! Should you make the time to teach Kitty not to run out the door? You bet you should!

6

❦ ❦ ❦

KITTY AEROBICS

KITTY CALISTHENICS AND
FELINE PHYSICAL FITNESS

EXERCISE ISN'T JUST
FOR FAT CATS

Kitty really doesn't need sweat socks or a jogging suit and she doesn't need to attend an aerobics class with an instructor yelling out ". . . and one and two and three and four." What she does need is her own personal fitness trainer—and you're it. It's up to you to be sure Kitty stays on the move long enough to get her heart pumping—at least three times a week. A sedentary life-style may very possibly infringe on the quality of her life and her health. If you don't use it, you lose it.

Any cat (providing the vet says he or she is healthy enough for exercise) should have the opportunities for stretching exercises, to get those muscles limber, and to get some aerobic exercise.

When Kitty looks and feels better, she'll better enjoy everything about life—including you. This means more hugging, kissing, and loving will come your way. Now what could be a better fringe benefit than that!

FAT CATS ARE A PRIORITY AND OWNERS
NEED TO CLEAN UP THEIR ACTS

"Kitty's too fat. I don't understand it." I must hear this from owners a dozen times a week. What's there to understand? Most kitties haven't yet learned to plug in the can opener, although I must admit I know a few who have figured out how to raid the refrigerator. For the most part, they are not the ones in charge of dispensing food. Only human family members are to blame when Kitty's eating habits get out of control (see page 187).

Insufficient exercise and overly sufficient food make for fat cats, chubby puppies, and puffy people. I don't care what diet is on this week's fad list, if Kitty's been proclaimed healthy by the vet, there's only one way he can get rid of a tubby tummy—and that's a combination of fewer calories and more activity.

PSYCHOLOGICAL WEAR AND TEAR

Psychologically it's not good for Kitty to bear the brunt of all those fat-cat jokes. Don't kid yourself into thinking those barbs don't hurt her feelings. Most pets know when you're talking about them and they can tell by the tone of your voice more or less what you're saying. It hurts Kitty's feelings when everyone laughs about her stomach leaving a trail of its own in the snow. She also knows the joke's on her when she leaps for the couch—and misses.

BIG NUMBERS AND BIG MEDICAL
PROBLEMS FOR FAT CATS

Statistics on the number of overweight cats vary. However, any way you look at it, too many kitties are packing away those extra pounds. It's important to keep your cat trim and svelte. Not only will she look and feel better about herself, the pressure and stress of the extra weight on Kitty's bones, muscles, and organs could actually be sending her to an early grave!

Every owner of every overweight cat I've ever met was

loving and caring and would hurdle the high jump to help his
or her precious fuzzy friend. It's beyond me why these same
owners can't make the connection that Kitty's extra weight
could be as injurious to her health as hundreds of other ailments
and diseases. Maybe they just don't think it can happen to their
cat.

TAKING ACTION

A healthy cat needs to remain active. All the dieting in the
world won't help weight loss the way dieting combined with
exercise will. Shedding pounds isn't complicated—it just
means that Kitty needs to burn off more calories than she's
taking in. Starving her through severe diets isn't right. Having
her eat healthy amounts of food and burn off the fat by working
out is better.

There are pages and pages of tips throughout this book on
how to help Kitty participate in life rather than simply sun
herself in the window. Encourage kitty activity. Build a kitty
condo (see page 115), take her for a stroll around the neighborhood, build a kitty gym (page 151). Do *something*. *Anything!* Just make sure Kitty gets up and starts moving.

CHECK WITH KITTY'S DOC

Before beginning any exercise program, be sure Kitty has a
physical checkup. Tell the vet Kitty's about ready to start an
exercise regimen. Certain age, weight, or medical problems
may cause the vet to place limits on or even nix your planned
approach to Kitty's fitness.

START SLOW AND DON'T OVERDO

Don't throw Kitty headfirst into an exercise program. Don't go
for the burn. Begin slowly, then very gradually increase the
program every couple of weeks. Please, no crash course for
Kitty. Don't try to make up for lost time—it could make her

sick or even kill her! Every cat is a little bit different, so check with the vet for guidelines. A lot depends on Kitty's present physical condition. Stop before there's heavy panting, and keep your eyes open for signs of too much physical stress, such as a darkening of the pink areas of the inner ears, tongue, gums, and eyes. Deeper pink or red tones could mean Kitty's over-exerted, and you could be doing more harm than good. Also, be alert to a grey color in those same areas. This too could be a trouble signal. When in doubt, stop.

BUILDING A KITTY GYM

Every cat-owning home should have a kitty gym . . . well, at least a kitty rec room . . . well, at least *part* of a room. Kitty doesn't need weights and an exercise bike but she does need enough indoor possibilities to keep her fit.

Use those boxes and bags I talked about earlier. Also, think about buying and installing shelf systems that allow Kitty to climb up to the ceiling (handy owners can build their own).

If Kitty's a swatter, think about creating a boxing gym for your little Mike Tyson. Plenty of cat toys come on strings. There's even a kitty fishing pole that you can dangle while Kitty punches away (Mowdy's personal favorite). Caution must be used with any toy that has an attached string, rope, or similar connecting part, as Kitty could become entangled and choke. Remove these toys when you're not around to supervise the activity.

Add some extra scratching paraphernalia to her exercise equipment.

Chasing after thrown toys is an easy way to get Kitty's heart pumping, so clear a path for a little indoor aerobics. You'll need a little space free of furniture and obstacles. Otherwise, Kitty could go skidding into the sofa. One run-in with the couch may be all it takes for her to decide she wants nothing to do with aerobic chasing.

FOR FELINE SPORTS
AFICIONADOS

Play kitty baseball if that's what she enjoys. Lots of cats like to pretend they're Babe Ruth and play batter up when a piece of crumbled paper is tossed their way.

If hockey's his game, by all means indulge him. You can forget about the ice, skates, nets, and protective head gear. Just find out what Kitty prefers to use as a puck. Grapes seem to be a popular choice; so do ice cubes. Both tend to mess up the floor so you may want to substitute something else. Whatever you choose, just be sure it's either large enough so it can't be swallowed or won't harm him if he should decide to eat it.

IMPORT A PHYSICAL FITNESS TRAINER
THAT JUST HAPPENS TO BE AN ANIMAL

If Kitty enjoys the company of other cats or dogs, set up regular meeting schedules. It's the easiest way to encourage kitty calisthenics. Owners can sit back and have a Danish and coffee (tsk, tsk on that Danish) while the pet pals chase around to their hearts' content. Just be sure Kitty's playmates are friendly towards other animals, healthy, and up to date on their vaccinations.

PUT ON YOUR THINKING CAP

There are so many ways to encourage Kitty to become and stay active. Anything that gets her up and moving will help keep her physically fit. Think long and hard about any participation games and exercises, but make sure there's nothing about them that could hurt your precious little furball. Don't overdo. You don't need your cat to look like a bodybuilder, you just need a healthy, happy kitty.

KITTY MASSAGE

There's nothing like a good massage, I'm sure you'll agree. And so will Kitty, once you get past the what-the-heck-are-you-doing-to-me stage.

The first few times I attempted to give Mowdy a massage, he took off like Superman—faster than a speeding bullet. But I stuck it out, believing that this one-time stray had probably never been touched or loved by human hands, and that when he got used to it he'd love it. Well, I was right. Now he's like a kid in a candy shop. He always wants more, more, more.

Kitty massage is the ultimate feline luxury and it costs you nothing. You can do it yourself.

WHY A MASSAGE?

Kitty massage has a lot of fringe benefits. Besides feeling good, a massage will help desensitize Kitty to being touched. He'll come to associate a wonderful, soothing, relaxed feeling with the human hands that massage him. This will carry over when Kitty needs to be touched, picked at or probed by you, the vet, or the groomer. No longer will Kitty assume touch is something from which to pull away.

A gentle rubdown also feels great to any pet suffering from a little arthritis; certain hip, leg or back problems; and some other forms of chronic pain. But always check with the vet to be sure Kitty's problems won't be aggravated by massage.

A good rubdown may calm a hyperactive cat and help create better behavior. Kitty could be so laid back after a massage that he might even want to take a . . . catnap. (Sorry, I just couldn't resist.)

Massage can substitute as a form of praise and positive reinforcement—one that Kitty will truly come to cherish. Being the recipient of such pleasant touching is good for Kitty's self-esteem. Your hands tell him you care.

There's one more great fringe benefit to Kitty massage—and this one's for you. Many recent medical studies indicate that people who stroke their pets are healthier and may even be able to reduce their own blood pressure!

Now that I've got your attention and you no longer think I'm crazy, let's get to it.

WHAT EVERY KITTY MASSEUR AND MASSEUSE SHOULD KNOW

At the risk of making my advice seem too easy I'm going to say this anyway: Almost any massage or rubbing technique will do. However, there are a few points that need to be considered before you start.

Cats are small and delicate so use an *extremely* light touch.

Stay clear of the spinal cord.

Check your technique with Kitty's doctor before her first massage. Be sure you're not about to do anything that might hurt her.

THE "HOW TO" OF THE KITTY MASSAGE TECHNIQUE

Now, begin the massage with a few minutes of general rubbing and stroking as you talk quietly to Kitty. Stroke the back of her neck and work your way to the tail. When you get to the hip area be extra gentle. From the hips, stroke down the rear legs to the paws. Now you can begin the real massage, using a circular motion of the fingers. Start just behind the head and do the neck, massaging the area in circles. Work your way down the back, staying away from the spinal cord, and keep rotating your fingers. Don't let your fingers break contact with Kitty's skin. Next, spend some time on her rear legs, kneading them like delicate bread dough. Don't make the pressure too hard— this is a sensitive area.

At the end of the massage, a good scratch all over is certainly in order.

If Kitty's never been too fond of extra touching, you'll need to take things slowly. Let her adjust to light strokes for a few days or weeks, then to a few seconds of massage. Talk to her. Coo over her. Your soothing voice will help communicate that she doesn't have to be afraid. Over time, build up to where she'll tolerate and then enjoy a more complete massage.

Now, wasn't that easy?

7

※　※　※

ON THE ROAD WITH AND WITHOUT KITTY

TRAVELING WITH KITTY

DON'T LEAVE HOME WITHOUT HIM

Are your well-deserved vacations spoiled because you just can't cope with the anxiety of leaving behind the little furball? Do you worry so much about Kitty's health and welfare that it's difficult to relax and have a good time? Or do you simply miss the comfort of his fuzzy little body?

When it comes to vacation time many cat owners make excuses to friends and family as to why they can't go away. They're afraid of becoming the target of ridicule for allowing cats to rule their lives. If friends and relatives have you thinking that there may be something wrong because your attachment to Kitty is unnatural—well, just stop thinking that this very instant! You're not alone. A lot of caring cat owners feel exactly the same way. Their cats are members of the family and they would no sooner take a family vacation without their cats than without their kids. Plenty of cat owners would love to pack up their little darlings and take them on a holiday, but they're afraid of the unknown, envisioning a catatonic Kitty totally stressed out from the journey and from being in a strange, new environment.

The flip side of the problem (unless you're one of the lucky people with a friend who just loves to take care of your cat *and* a cat who just loves to be taken care of by your friend) is to leave Kitty with the vet or at a kennel/cattery (see page 177). However, for many of us, the choice of steel cages, barking dogs, yowling cats, and care provided by strangers is not a viable solution—no matter how professional and perfect the boarding facility may be.

THE SOLUTION

Well, you don't have to leave home without him! You can take Kitty on your trip as long as you make special arrangements for your four-footed vacationer. It's hectic just before a trip and there are always a million things to do. Make a checklist or refer to this chapter when vacation time rolls around. You don't want to get caught short, particularly when you are caring for something that's so dependent upon your organizational skills.

SAFEGUARD THE CAT'S HEALTH AND WELFARE

Before the trip, arrange for Kitty to have a medical check-up. While you're at the animal hospital get a health certificate stating that Kitty has been known to the vet for a number of years (if that's the case), is in good health, and is up-to-date on her vaccinations. Inquire with the state, country, or transportation carrier as to how close to the time of travel the pet must be examined (a good travel agent will also be able to give you the proper information). A health certificate from six months ago will not be sufficient. Kitty will need a health certificate when crossing borders into other countries and prior to airline travel, even on domestic flights (although they often fail to ask to see it at check-in time).

Be sure to have your veterinarian's phone number with you. Also, bring along any prescription drugs Kitty's required to take and an extra prescription that can be filled, or at least referred to, by a vet licensed to practice in your vacation area.

TWO FORMS OF ID, PLEASE

For underaged kids trying to sneak into bars, the most dreaded words in the world are "two forms of ID please." The policy of requiring two forms of ID may prevent youngsters from entering a bar, and it can help safeguard Kitty, too. While traveling, things tend to fall off or break, so be equipped with some extra kitty ID—one tag for the collar and another packed away to replace the original if necessary. Put your phone number on the tag, as well as that of your vet, or someone else you can count on. Remember, you and your family will be out of town, so if Kitty gets lost no one will be at home to answer the phone.

While you're doubling up on equipment, toss in an extra collar, harness, leash, or whatever is used by your cat.

HUSH-A-BYE AND SWEET DREAMS

If you want your little furball to quickly settle into his new space, be sure to pack either his bed, favorite pillow, security blanket, or special towel. Even if your cat can fall asleep anywhere, anytime, having his special little blanky along will add to his sense of well-being.

HAVE TOYS, WILL TRAVEL

It's equally important to pack some of the cat's toys. Playing with a few old favorites may be just the trick to help maintain Kitty's sense of security while he adjusts to a new environment. Pack a few new ones, too. When you break out all these goodies, he'll associate his vacation home with having a great time.

WHERE WILL KITTY SLEEP?

Better yet, where will the owners sleep? Don't be afraid you won't have anywhere to stay if you bring Kitty along. It's up to the management of each hotel within most chains to set the pet policy, and a fair percentage allows cats. If you run out of luck with the major hotels, try bed and breakfast hotels (or should that be Bed and Whiskers Hotels?). Sometimes their policies are more flexible. In any case, call ahead and, if necessary, offer to sign an agreement holding you responsible for any damage Kitty might do. You might also offer to forward an additional security deposit.

When you check out after a successful stay, try to get a letter from the management describing your cat's good behavior. If you manage to collect a few letters over the years it will certainly help ease your way into hotels with stricter pet policies.

Several years ago (when hotel policies were more rigid) I did a lot of traveling with a pet I had educated to respond to certain common courtesies. Inevitably, hotel managers would want to meet my four-footed traveling companion before we registered. As the manager made his way over to us, I'd look him square in the eyes and when he got close enough I'd thrust out my hand with a confident hand shake. Then I'd use my little secret weapon. "Binky," I'd say, "shake hands with the manager." Binky would oblige, extending his paw for the most adorable handshake. It worked every time.

After you've arrived at the hotel, even if you're tired, carry the cat's container to the room yourself. A ride on the bellhop's cart can be a little bumpier than Kitty might like.

It's never a good idea to leave a cat alone in a hotel room (some hotels don't even allow it), but if you must, call the front desk *and* housekeeping. Notify everyone not to come into the room, and hang the DO NOT DISTURB sign on the door. Besides theft, the big concern is that someone entering the room will allow the cat to escape out the door. You might consider leaving the cat secured in the carrier or blocking the area around the door. That way, if someone should walk in, Kitty won't bolt out of the room.

A KITTY KIT FOR FELINE FIRST-AID

Packing a first-aid kit for the animal kids is a must! Cats in new environments tend to be curious and their instincts to explore might get them into something more than they bargained for. They're more apt to experiment with foreign objects on the ground, so be sure to read about the Heimlich maneuver on page 195. There's also a strong possibility of an upset stomach or other illness occurring due to the stress of traveling. *Remember:* First aid is only an immediate, temporary, emergency measure until a veterinarian can be consulted.

For Kitty's first-aid kit, take along:

gauze
bandages
diarrhea and stomach-upset preparations. Include a note with
the vet's recommended dose.
unbreakable rectal thermometer (normal temperature is approximately 101.5, plus or minus 1 degree, depending on
the individual cat, time of day, and recent activity level)
petroleum jelly for easier thermometer insertion
insect-bite stick
flea and tick products
wound disinfectant
scissors
tweezers

HELP AVOID TUMMY UPSETS

A change of diet, water, and environment certainly increases the risk of Kitty having a topsy-turvy tummy (and your doing the type of cleaning up you didn't envision for your vacation). To help avoid kitty upset stomachs, bring enough water from home for the entire trip or at least a sufficient supply to gradually wean Kitty onto the new water. Also, check to see if Kitty's usual brand of food is available at your destination, as well as any stops along the way. If it is not, try to pack up as much of it as possible. If you're leaving the country, be sure to check with customs officials about whether you can bring Kitty's food and water with you.

TAKE CARE OF BOTH ENDS

Don't forget about the necessary equipment for the mouth and the tush. If Kitty's food dishes at home are unbreakable (which they should be), bring them along. For experienced traveling cats, a few clean half-pound margarine containers can be used as dishes. They'll generally do the trick and won't add much weight to the baggage. If Kitty eats canned food, take a can opener. Almost everyone forgets this little appliance.

Pack Kitty's litter box and her favorite litter. Many cats are comfortable only in their own john and would rather die than use an unfamiliar litter or litter box. If your cat isn't fussy, many pet stores carry folding, portable cardboard litter boxes. They work and they're easy to carry. Be sure you can purchase your regular litter at your destination. If not, lug it along.

SHOULD KITTY HAVE HER OWN SUITCASE?

If by now you're thinking there's so much kitty stuff that the furball needs her own suitcase, you're right—unless you have a lot of room left over in yours. Stop to think about it. Your cat is a living, breathing member of the family and just because she's smaller than everyone else, it doesn't mean she shouldn't receive the same considerations as other family members.

TO FEED OR NOT TO FEED,
THAT IS THE BIG QUESTION

Much of the recommended advice on whether to feed Kitty prior to travel suggests no food for as many as six to twelve hours beforehand. I don't follow that advice unless I find that a particular cat does best that way. Although I cut back on the food intake ahead of time (there's no sense in risking a queasy full stomach or making Kitty uncomfortable because she needs to eliminate), I find that most cats do best when they have a small bland snack before traveling. A snack seems to help absorb stomach acid that might otherwise sour Kitty's already stressed travel tummy.

Leaving water in the carrier is another consideration. While it's nice for Kitty to have drinking water at her disposal, 9.9 times out of 10 the water spills in transport and Kitty has to take a wet ride. There are waterers available that only dispense water when licked. If Kitty gets the hang of using one (at first you might try smearing it with some of her favorite food to encourage her to lick it), let her travel with it.

PREVENTING CAR CHAOS

Car travel requires cats to be willing passengers within the confines of an automobile. Before setting out on your journey, be sure Kitty feels comfortable being in the car. I'll give you some tips later in this chapter to help ensure a happy trip.

CAN KITTY FLY?

I want you to know I've resisted adding any number of terrible jokes about flying cats. With that said, the answer is yes, cats can fly, by plane. Kitty has a big advantage over all but the smallest of dogs as he can travel with you in the cabin. He doesn't have to experience the less glamorous cargo section.

Make reservations well in advance. Most airlines limit the number of pets allowed in each cabin per flight. Also, be sure Kitty is adjusted to a cat carrier that's approved for airline travel (see page 171). On the carrier put a label with your phone number and an emergency phone number both on the outside *and* the inside, just in case the outer label rips off. Also, never tie a leash or rope around the carrier, or use an ID label that ties on to the carrier. It could fall inside and Kitty could become entangled in it and choke to death.

Line the bottom of the carrier with something soft and absorbent. Try biodegradable disposable diapers if you're positive Kitty won't attempt to eat them. Pack extra carrier lining material in a bag you're taking on board. If Kitty has a potty accident you can quickly change the lining in the bathroom, or if the seat belt sign is on and you're prevented from getting up, at least the urine will settle into the lining, keeping Kitty comfy and eliminating some of the odor.

Some cats are so perfect about using litter boxes, their owners bring them on board and discreetly take cat and box to the bathroom. Bingo!—Kitty knows what to do. If that's your kitty, be sure the litter can be flushed in the toilet, or bring along enough bags to wrap and dispose of the litter so that offensive odors can't escape.

FLYING IN AND OUT

Always try to book a direct flight. With stopovers and plane changes there are greater risks for human error if the cat isn't traveling with you in the cabin. I'm sure you've heard the stories about disappearing luggage. What if that were Kitty?

Keep temperatures in mind when scheduling landing and departure times, particularly if Kitty is traveling in cargo. When traveling to a hot climate, schedule your arrival and departure for the cooler times of early morning or late evening. This will help reduce the risk of harm to a cat who's been accidentally left in a hot area during loading or unloading, or—heaven forbid—who's trapped if the carrier gets lost. Do the opposite when traveling to cold climates, and schedule your traveling times during the warmer times of day.

WATCH OUT FOR THOSE QUARANTINE LAWS

Always inquire about a country's quarantine laws—some countries have them and some don't. In 1989, Liza Minnelli unknowingly ran afoul of Swedish law for not observing animal quarantine requirements.

Sometimes even different areas of the same country have variations on the quarantine law. For instance, in the United States, Hawaii has a quarantine for pets coming in from the other states as well as from foreign countries.

SPREAD YOUR MONEY AROUND

If you must send your cat via the pressurized cargo area (which I don't recommend unless it absolutely can't be avoided), don't be cheap. Tip, tip, and tip again any airport personnel who might be handling the cat carrier.

Wait until the last possible minute to send Kitty off to the baggage area. You might be told over the phone that she has to be loaded one or more hours before departure. While you certainly should arrive by the appointed time, once you're at the counter, animal-loving airline personnel will often let you wait until the last twenty minutes before saying good-bye to her.

TRAVELING ON TRAINS AND BUSES

Kitty may not be welcome on trains and buses. Check ahead of time. Some countries are more flexible than others. The United States is tough, but France is fairly flexible. If Kitty is able to ride the rails or bus, be sure to follow all the same safety steps as with other forms of travel.

ONE CAT OR TWO?

If you're traveling with two cats, you might be tempted to squeeze them both into one carrier. *Don't do it,* even in a larger carrier. Apart from some airlines not allowing it, it can make traveling more difficult. Unless the cats are really great buddies or so insecure they need each other's companionship, it may be very hard for them to tolerate such close confinement. You may find that tight quarters are enough to fray their nerves and cause nasty behavior. Any husband and wife traveling together have probably experienced those very same emotions. Of course, *I* wouldn't know about that. All my traveling experiences have been wonderful, haven't they, dear?

TRANQUILIZERS—SHOULD KITTY HAVE HER OWN PILLBOX?

Cat tranquilizers are a hot subject of debate. I don't use them with my cats. I prefer to take the lengthier route of ensuring my cats are well-adjusted to the rigors of travel. Tranquilized cats must deal with both the stress of the trip and the drugged feelings that can't be explained to them. Some even suffer side effects.

Although I've never owned a pet who couldn't adjust to travel without tranquilizers, I can appreciate that some cats and owners simply can't get the hang of traveling without them. So, if you think Kitty needs to be lulled into traveling, ask your vet for a prescription.

PSYCHOLOGICALLY DESENSITIZE KITTY

SPECIAL TIPS FOR FRIGHTENED FELINES AND FIRST-TIME TRAVELERS

If Kitty's never traveled before, or if you suspect she may be frightened, there are some extra steps to take. Try them as an alternative to tranquilizers.

If Kitty's going to be a jet-set pet for the first time or you know she's nervous about flying, take her to the airport before the trip. This will give her the chance to get used to the hustle and bustle. It will help her sensitive ears adjust to the noise of people and planes and allow her nose to adjust to the odor of jet fuel.

If extra trips to the airport are out of the question, at least get a sound-effects recording of crowd noises and planes taking off and landing. Play the recording at a low volume. As Kitty becomes accustomed to the volume over a period of weeks, gradually increase the level. The same can be done for car travel by purchasing a recording of automobile and truck noises.

POTTY ETIQUETTE

If Kitty has been trained to walk on a leash, please walk him away from the hotel grounds and always scoop up the poop. If Kitty's using a litter box in the room, be extra meticulous about its cleanliness. While you may be desensitized to that little extra cat odor, others may not. If the litter can't be flushed down the toilet, don't just dump it in the pail in the room and have someone else get stuck cleaning it up. That's what gives traveling pets a bad name. Wrap it up well and ask management for the location of the outside dumpster. We shouldn't expect others to do our cats' dirty work.

WATER SPORTS, ANYONE?

If boating is on your itinerary, be sure to purchase a life preserver made especially for cats. Yes, they really do make them but you'll probably have to track one down at a pet specialty or novelty store. Adjust the cat to the life preserver well in advance. (Read pages 129–30 again, and follow the directions, substituting the preserver for the leash and harness.)

When Kitty's on a boat, be sure he has access to a shaded area, is restrained with a leash, and is supervised at all times by owners taking nothing for granted when it comes to the safety of the cat.

Fishermen must take note that fishhooks hurt a lot when lodged in delicate paws and skin. It may not even be your fault but the temptation of something shiny and wiggly at the end of fishing line might be more than Kitty can resist. In a flash, that little mouser of a feline could pounce and *ouch*—there's going to be a big problem.

Soda pop, beer, and juice are not on the recommended list for keeping Kitty from getting thirsty when he's out on the water. Don't forget to bring along a kitty thermos filled with cool water.

Keep in mind all the precautions in this section if your leisure time will be spent around a pool, lake, a beach, or just near the docks. Also, hot sand can hurt tender feet, particularly of those cats accustomed to life on a padded carpet.

IS EVERYBODY READY TO GO?
So when you're packing and discover your precious little furball is sitting in your suitcase with upset, soulful eyes, remember—you don't have to leave home without her!

HAPPY CAR TRAVEL—
ADJUSTING KITTY TO THE CAR
AND COPING WITH CAR SICKNESS

Hooray! No more cat screeching. No more cat claws embedded in the back of your neck, and no more carsick cats. Kitty can be taught to ride in an automobile like the well-mannered feline you know she is. She can be taught not only to tolerate car travel but to actually love it. You may not believe it now, but the time will come when Kitty will look forward to your rides together.

THE BIG MISTAKE
Don't fall into the trap of putting Kitty in the car only when she needs to go to the vet's office. Think about it: If the only time

you rode in a car was to go to the doctor to have your body probed and to receive a shot with a big, long needle, you'd be a bit cranky about getting into the car yourself. I know you'd have to drag me in kicking and screaming.

For most cats their only experience with cars is negative and associated with stress. How can we possibly expect them to know the difference when we decide to take them on an occasional car trip? When Kitty sees the car, as far as she's concerned, it's doctor time again. She's smart enough to put two and two together and she says, "Good-bye. Thanks but no thanks, I'm heading under the bed. Just try to get me out of here."

If you begin training your cat to enjoy car travel, and not just use the car as a means of transport to the vet's office, you'll be able to plan some terrific vacations that include Kitty. You may even find yourself in an emergency situation and have to take her in the car for an extended length of time. Let me tell you about something that happened to Mowdy and me.

MOWDY'S MAJOR CAR EXPERIENCE
I gained a whole new respect for Mowdy when, due to circumstances beyond my control, I thrust him and his dog brother, Tige, into a traveling situation that warranted giving them medals for excellence. I was expected to be in Orlando, Florida, to appear on a television show at Disney/MGM studios in Disney World. It was a brand-new facility then (the official grand opening hadn't even taken place), and it was the first week of taping for *The New Mickey Mouse Club*. I am the club's "creature keeper" and was doing a segment with a stageful of Dalmatians—sort of a takeoff of the Disney movie *101 Dalmations*. The taping was on Wednesday and I had tickets for a Tuesday flight. On Monday, New York suffered a major snowstorm, which meant major delays at the airports. On top of that, a pilot's strike was in effect at one of the airlines, and there was some talk that pilots from other carriers

were going to honor it. Well, there was no way I was going to miss that taping. I'm a baby boomer and grew up with *The Mickey Mouse Club*. Being a part of *The New Mickey Mouse Club* was my little piece of television history. So, at 9:00 P.M. Monday night, I loaded up the cat, the dog, and my wife (not necessarily in that order), got into my four-wheel-drive truck, and off we went—slowly. The snow and subsequent ice storm lasted all the way through Virginia. I figured we'd have to drive through the night but also that we'd get to Florida in time to relax in the late afternoon and get a really good night's sleep. Fat chance. Because of the storm it took nine hours to travel the first three hundred miles. My little four-footed passengers, Mowdy and Tige, took it in stride.

Then somewhere around Savannah, Georgia, I got a toothache the likes of which I had never felt before. Even though I was crazy with pain, I decided to tough it out. Three quarters of the way through Georgia I realized that if I didn't have something done very quickly I was going to rip the tooth out myself. Mowdy and Tige weren't sure what my bizarre behavior was all about but those two little angels knew something was wrong, so they sat ever so still, not even asking to go for a walk.

Now we're in the middle of I-don't-know-where, Georgia. The next big city is Jacksonville, Florida. I'm screaming with pain. At ten o'clock Tuesday night—twenty-five hours after we started—we located a dentist willing to see some stranger off the street. Mowdy and his brother continued to behave like angels. Well, I got all shot up with Novocain and got a couple of prescriptions to help me through the next few days. Luckily we found a pharmacy that was open till midnight. The cat and dog were still behaving as good as gold. Off we continued to Orlando which, unbeknownst to me, was still three hours away.

We finally rolled in at 3:00 A.M.—thirty hours after we left New York. We had to be at the television studio at seven in the morning so, after only three hours' sleep, we got up, packed up

Mowdy and Tige one more time, and went to the studio. Those two darlings stayed with only a few walks in the dressing room all day. We didn't finish until six o'clock that night. Mowdy and Tige didn't miss a beat—no accidents and no whimpering or crying. I would have understood if they had never spoken to me again. But, of course, they did understand and didn't hold a grudge. What can I say about my little guys? They're great. We had a family experience we can all look back on and laugh about. But, if it wasn't for Mowdy and Tige's car-riding skills, things could have been a *lot* worse.

TAKING KITTY ON VACATION

Even cats that do well on a five-minute ride to the beach may have an entirely different opinion of a five-hour ride to va-cationland. Few cats would tolerate what Mowdy went through. In psychological lingo, it's called flooding — throwing too much at Kitty all at once. So build up to it slowly. Even cats who are car lovers may need some training for longer rides.

KITTY NEEDS TO BUCKLE UP

Before Kitty goes for any car ride, his safety and the safety of other passengers must be considered. Kitty should be restrained in one form or another. A restraining device needs to serve two purposes. Heaven forbid there's an accident or even an abrupt stop, Kitty could become a flying furball, thrown about or even out of the car like a limp rag doll. If the impact doesn't hurt— or kill—him, his fright might cause him to run off, never to be seen again. Second, it is equally important to prevent Kitty from interfering with the driver in any way or from working his way onto the floor, where he might become wedged in around the gas and brake pedals. I know of more than one accident that occurred while a frantic driver tried to untangle Kitty from the floorboards.

FIRST, THERE'S A DECISION TO MAKE

When choosing a restraining device, there are several options to consider. Some owners like it if Kitty rides in a cat carrier. Others don't like the confinement of a carrier, choosing instead to educate their cats to sit still in a cat seat belt (yes, they really do make them. Would I kid you?). Still others prefer to have a passenger hold Kitty on a leash and harness.

If you decide on the leash and harness or a seat belt, read the information on pages 129–30 again. (The same advice for acclimating Kitty to a leash and harness can be followed for a seat belt.) If a seat belt is your choice, you might be able to find one at a pet shop that carries novelty and specialty items.

SELECTING A CARRIER

What to do, what to do? It's so confusing. There are so many types of cat carriers on the market. Most people don't have a clue as to which one to choose and are often misled by salespeople who may or may not have the appropriate knowledge to make such purchase suggestions. Much of your decision should be based on the nature of your travel needs. There are pros and cons for almost any selection. Final approval, however, rests with Kitty. If she doesn't like it everyone's stuck.

THINK AHEAD

When you're plunking down your hard earned money on a carrier, buy one that fits all your possible needs, not just for the car travel you have in mind today but the air travel that might take place in the future. Buy the right carrier now and you won't have to buy or rent another one later. So my first suggestion is to buy a carrier that's suitable for car travel and is also approved for use by the airlines. The ones I like best are fairly standard and made of molded plastic. Be sure the carrier is designed to fit under an airplane seat. Airlines vary in their size restrictions for cat carriers so be sure your choice meets the standards for most of them.

WHEN OTHER CARRIERS WILL DO JUST FINE

If your fear of flying precludes any possibility of your cat entering the world of jet setters, then other types of carriers will serve the needs of car travel. Make sure the carrier is sturdy. Be a good consumer—check around the seams and locks, and for rough edges that could hurt Kitty. Test the effectiveness of the locking system. Also check the handle or carrying strap. Has it been attached with double stitching or an extra set of grommets for added strength? Are there sufficient openings to allow good ventilation? Although wicker types are attractive I'm always fearful something will come apart when I least expect it. If you'd prefer a shoulder bag that Kitty just pops into, be sure it has enough support on the bottom and enough to hold up the sides. Insufficient support can cause Kitty to get all scrunched up while riding along on your shoulder, and when the bag is placed on the floor the unsupported sides just cave in around the little tyke.

Some cats love carriers with clear plastic tops; since some kitties are nosy, they wouldn't be happy unless they could see everything that's going on around them. For shy or less secure cats this is frightening—any carrier allowing them to see too much passing scenery is psychologically over-whelming. Also, clear plastic tops offer no protection from the sun. Even the winter sun beating down on Kitty through the car windows can create too much heat.

Check out a variety of different carriers before you make a choice but rule out the cardboard versions. They don't offer nearly the security I demand when traveling with such precious kitty cargo.

ENSURING A GOOD FIT—HOW BIG IS
BIG AND HOW BIG IS TOO BIG?

The rule of thumb is that Kitty should have enough room for the length of her body and then some, as well as for her height, again with a little to spare. Kitty must be able to get up and turn around in order to get comfortable. But don't be fooled into trying to be kind by providing an extra large carrier for Kitty's trip. Too much extra space inside the carrier means Kitty will be thrown about as she slips and slides during her transport.

GETTING KITTY COMFY IN THE CARRIER

Visions of getting Kitty into a carrier sometimes resemble really bad nightmares. There's Kitty screaming away with all four paws pushing out in different directions as you try to wrestle her into the carrier's opening. You're hoping that once you get her in she won't pop out before you close the door. You're also hoping all of this gets done with no bloodshed— hers or yours. Of course, if Kitty's clever or has been through this before, she'll take one look at the carrier and *adiós*—she's out of there, speeding under the bed in record-setting time. I'm sure a lot of you know this scenario. But it doesn't have to be that way.

Don't dump a carrier on little Kitty all at once. Take it one step at a time. First, leave the carrier in an area where she spends a lot of time. Keep the top open or, in the case of a screw-on top, take it off. Place something soft and comfy on the bottom so she's not forced to lie on a hard, cool surface. Put some of her favorite toys and treats in there, too. Then leave things alone.

Don't bring her over to the carrier and don't react to it. Just leave it on the floor for a week or two (or longer for cats who are really frightened of carriers) until you see that she just considers it part of your home's decor.

When Kitty no longer thinks twice about walking past the

carrier or poking her little curious nose into it, spend a few seconds here and there putting her into it. Don't try to restrain her. If she wants to jump out right away, let her. Use a lot of praise before, during, and right after the carrier experience. Let Kitty think that whenever the carrier is near she'll receive so much positive attention that all this carrier stuff is the best thing that's ever happened to her.

Don't rush. You have nothing to lose by going slowly—and everything to lose by going too quickly. When everything seems okay, repeat the procedure, but this time close the top for a second or two. Open it quickly and let Kitty jump out. Make it a game of hide and seek or peekaboo, complete with your most excited "play" voice. If the carrier is the type that you've been able to completely unscrew the top, now's the time to put it on before you put Kitty in the carrier. Leave the door open so she can come right out at her own choosing. Once she's comfortable with that, you can move on to closing the door for a second or two. Continue playing the hide and seek and peekaboo games.

Once you've gotten this far the rest is easy. Gradually increase the amount of time Kitty spends in the carrier. Take it nice and slow, building in increments of a few minutes at a time. Always have the carrier filled with Kitty's favorite food and toys and make a big fuss over her. If Kitty associates great things with the carrier, you'll be well on your way to happy traveling.

TRAVELING BY
STATION WAGON OR VAN

If you plan on driving in a van or station wagon you might consider traveling light and making room for one of the large cat cages on the market. Such cages are big enough for the litter box, a bed, some toys, and all the comforts of home. The only disadvantage is that if the car comes to an abrupt stop there's a lot of room in which Kitty can be thrown about.

DESENSITIZE
KITTY TO THE CAR

Regardless of whether Kitty's a novice car rider, is terrorized of the car or tolerates the car without really enjoying it, the steps to desensitizing her are the same. Whatever you do, don't just stick Kitty in the car, start the engine, and go off on your merry way—unless you want to risk trauma and a carsick kitty. Whenever you're dealing with—or trying to avoid—a feline psychological problem, it's best to break down the problem into the smallest possible parts and then deal with each part one at a time.

TINY LITTLE KITTY CAR STEPS

First, to minimize risk, put Kitty in the car using whatever restraining device you've chosen. Leave the car doors open. It's important that Kitty adjusts to the car without feeling restricted by being in a closed vehicle. After a few seconds take her back in the house. Before, during, and right after this process use lots and lots of praise, hugging, and kissing.

Once Kitty thinks her quick in and out of the car is no big deal, do the same thing with the doors closed. After a minute or two open the doors, bring her back into the house, and, as always, use plenty of praise and love.

Next, put Kitty in the car with the doors closed and start the engine. Let it run for a minute or so, shut it off, and take her back in the house, again using plenty of exaggerated enthusiasm. If you notice that the sound of the engine sets her back dramatically, tape-record the sound and play it in the house at progressively louder volumes until she adjusts to the noise. Do the same for traffic noise if Kitty finds it upsetting.

Be prepared to play the recordings for a week or two, and longer if necessary.

Now that you've accomplished all this I bet you think you're ready to go for a ride. Well, you're right. It's time to ride up and down the driveway or half a block or so. After this, turn around and drive right back home. Take this step gradually. The motion of a moving vehicle could be more than what Kitty's ready for. As she adjusts, increase the length of a ride to one complete block, then around the neighborhood. If Kitty has a favorite friend living close by, take her to the friend. Stopping the car for fun things will help break up the trip and she'll also associate the car with positive activities. If Kitty is leash and harness trained, bring her to an area you think she'll enjoy. As you progress you could even think about taking her on a picnic. Whatever you choose, the idea remains the same: Let Kitty think that being in the car means fun and exciting things are going to happen.

WON'T THIS TAKE A LONG TIME?

This all may sound like a lot of work but it really doesn't take more than a few minutes each day. When you stop to think of all the problems good car travel solves, it's well worth the effort. I know I don't have to convince anyone who's already lived through the experience of traveling with a cat who hates the carrier, the car, and everything else that goes along with it. Cats like that don't even get to the vet regularly—the stress seems to jeopardize their health and emotional well-being. It's worth the time to ensure your cat's happy response.

The process may be slow. If your cat is grown, fear may already be instilled in her. Just don't fall into the trap of thinking you can't teach an older cat new things. Give her more credit than that.

NEVER, NEVER, NEVER ...

Never allow Kitty to hang his head out the window of a moving car. Kitty may love it but road debris can lodge in his eyes, ears, and nose. A quick leap can also turn into an escape with a fatal ending.

Never leave a leash or rope on or in the carrier. It could strangle Kitty.

Never leave Kitty unattended in a car. Pet thievery is on the rise. Also, in warm temperatures, deadly conditions can occur in seconds. Cars parked in the shade are not exempt. As the sun moves, the shaded area changes. Be extra careful of cats with "pushed-in" faces (such as the Persian/Himalayan breeds). Due to their facial construction they are even more susceptible than other cats to hot temperatures in the car. And in cold weather cars turn into freezers—in no time.

C'MON KITTY, LET'S GO
Once Kitty's adjusted to the car he can see the vet regularly. He can go see Grandma or his sisters and brothers. He can go on a picnic or to a party. He can go on vacation.

CHOOSING A BOARDING FACILITY

TIPS FOR STAYING OUT OF TROUBLE
If you've decided that Kitty must stay behind when you go away there are things you must know.

Years ago I owned and operated a boarding facility for pets. I know firsthand what can happen in even the best-run facilities. Taking care of pets is like taking care of lots of little kids; no matter how careful you try to be, things happen. So to limit the risk of problems occurring, follow the steps I've put together for you.

Make personal inspections of facilities and stop in unannounced.

Visit a number of facilities and get educated. By making comparisons you'll be better prepared to make a decision.

Insist on seeing where the pets are kept, not just the reception room.

Arrive as early in the morning as you are allowed. This will give you an idea of the type of care the pets receive overnight. You'll also see how quick the staff is to feed and clean up after them in the morning.

Will Kitty's cage be adequate enough for her to move around in and feel comfortable?

Although it's important to meet and evaluate the receptionist and the owner/manager of the facility, it's equally (and perhaps even more) important to meet the workers in the kennel/cattery area. These are the people who will be in daily contact with your pet, and the quality of care will depend on them.

Check for cleanliness, not only in the middle of the floor but in the corners, too. Animal boarding facilities are perfect places for viral and bacterial problems to take hold. Personnel should always be on the lookout for dirt and hair buildup.

Will the facility provide the diet Kitty eats at home? If the answer is yes, take a look at the area where meals are prepared and verify that they have a variety of foods on hand. If the kennel or cattery will not provide the food, will you be allowed to supply it?

Does the boarding facility ask for written proof of vaccinations or at least insist on speaking to Kitty's vet to verify her shots? It's a problem if personnel is willing to take your word for it. You may be telling the truth, but other owners may not be or they may be confused as to the date of the last vaccinations.

Is there a vet on call in case of emergency? If so, who? Is the vet someone you trust? Will they call your vet?

Did the receptionist ask you to fill out a questionnaire asking for pertinent information, such as a number where you could be reached, the name and telephone number of a close friend or relative in case of emergency, a favorite food to perk up Kitty's appetite in case she's stressed and isn't eating, allergies to food, medication or insect bites, etc.?

Will the facility accept Kitty's mat or bed from home? They

should. Don't wash it before the boarding stay—it should carry the family's scent so Kitty doesn't feel so abandoned.

How much extra fencing is around the premises? What about double sets of doors? If Kitty were to get loose, would she have an easy time getting out of the building or is it designed to contain an escapee? Sooner or later every boarding facility experiences a pet getting out of its cage. The question is, if the pet is loose can it get out of the building?

Tip the workers before you leave on your trip. Be generous. It may help ensure some extra TLC for Kitty. Tip again when you return.

If you're going away for more than a week, be sure to have someone who knows Kitty stop into the facility to see her. Someone you trust should check for any obvious weight problems or illness.

As an extra safeguard, call from wherever you are and speak to the owner or manager. Even if it's a $5.00 phone call, it's worth the expense.

Don't be duped into thinking that if you've found someone who will board Kitty in their own home everything will be hunky-dory. Take all the steps I've already described for the larger facility. Remember, this person has opened up his or her home for business, so don't be shy about requesting an inspection of the entire place. Look at back rooms, basements, and attics. Often, a pet is locked away the moment the owner's out the door.

If you're lucky enough to have someone come in to your home to take care of Kitty, be just as careful as you would with any other boarding decision. Kitty's nanny should stop in a minimum of once a day (actually, two to three visits a day is really rock bottom as far as I'm concerned). At least one visit per day should be on the long side, so Kitty can have some playtime and special attention. Be sure the nanny knows about Kitty trying to sneak out the door. I can't begin to tell you how many friends or relatives have never forgiven themselves when the kitty in their charge escaped out the door, gone forever.

A TEARFUL GOOD-BYE

Of course you'll worry if Kitty's left behind, but sometimes we just don't have any choice in these matters. Try not to feel too guilty. If you take the time and do all your boarding homework, Kitty should be just fine.

8

❁ ❁ ❁

KITTY'S HEALTH-
INSURANCE PLAN

CAT DENTISTRY

When I first started talking about cat dentistry in the early 1970s I was the absolute laughingstock of the pet world. When I went on live television in the early 1980s extolling the benefits of brushing pets' teeth the pet industry as a whole still hadn't caught up to me.

Finally, things are beginning to change—and not a second too soon! Some statistics now show that 90 percent of all pets have some form of tooth or gum disease by the time they reach five years of age. That's horrendous!

What can you do to save Kitty's teeth from suffering the same dental fate? Brush them.

BRUSHING KITTY'S TEETH AT HOME

Breaking up plaque is the main ingredient to keep Kitty's mouth healthy. Brushing with a child's toothbrush or rubbing the teeth and gums with a washcloth or some gauze will do just fine. Any moderately abrasive action will help dislodge plaque.

WILL KITTY REMEMBER TO PUT THE CAP BACK ON
THE TOOTHPASTE?

Be careful when choosing a toothpaste. Don't use human toothpaste on cats—it can have negative effects, such as upsetting the stomach. Instead, speak to your vet about using baking soda, a baking soda/hydrogen peroxide combination, or a toothpaste made especially for cats (yes, it really does exist—I don't make these things up).

WILL KITTY TOLERATE YOUR DENTAL DOINGS?

However, don't expect the average kitty to greet you with open arms, or paws, when it comes to brushing her teeth. I don't know too many young kids that get a thrill out of brushing their teeth, either. However, as time goes on, most of those kids get used to the idea and find brushing more agreeable. Kitty won't get to the point of being able to brush and floss her own teeth, but she will start to let you brush them for her.

Don't even think about any mouth-cleaning attempts unless Kitty is thoroughly adjusted to being handled. If she's the type that won't even tolerate being held on your lap, you're certainly not ready for kitty dentistry. But if she's come to trust your handling of her or if you've gained better control over her from applying some of the educational techniques in this book, you're ready to roll.

TIPS TO HELP THE NO-WAY-AM-I-GOING-TO-SIT-STILL-FOR-THIS KITTY

Forget about brushing for a while and just get Kitty used to having your hands around his mouth. Use a few treats or a little kitty massage so that he comes to understand that your hands being around his mouth doesn't pose a threat.

Leave the toothbrush, washcloth, or a small piece of gauze around his toys or sleeping area for a week or two. Let him come to see it in a nonthreatening way.

If Kitty still looks like he'd rather die than have his teeth brushed, try putting some chicken soup, a little beef bouillon, or even some specially flavored cat food on the brushing apparatus.

The idea is to place one of Kitty's favorite foods on the tooth-brush, cloth, or gauze. Most cats are a lot more receptive when they associate the brushing utensil with something great tasting.

If necessary, start with a slow and gentle pass at the mouth and lips, and don't even think about going inside the mouth until Kitty seems relaxed about the whole affair.

When you're ready to brush the teeth, do it only for a second or two. Stop and offer Kitty a tremendous amount of praise. After every five or ten attempts increase the amount of time spent brushing by a few seconds.

DOES KITTY HAVE TO BRUSH AFTER EVERY MEAL?
Kitty doesn't need to have her teeth done two, three, or four times a day. However, once a day would be nice. If you can't manage that, at least try to work it in every other day.

WILL SHE GARGLE?
No, but she may bite or scratch. This is not meant to scare you—it simply means that if you haven't followed the necessary prerequisite steps for socializing and handling Kitty, don't expect things to fall into place. Only owners who have developed a mutual trust with their cat will be successful at good oral hygiene for Kitty.

THAT'S IT, RIGHT?
Wrong. Kitty still needs dental care provided by the vet. Polishing and professional cleaning are important. Without it, Kitty may end up like the vast majority of cats who suffer tooth loss and gum disease.

WHAT'S THE BIG DEAL IF KITTY HAS SOME DENTAL PROBLEMS AS SHE GETS OLDER?
It's a *very* big deal if Kitty's oral needs aren't met. Infection of the mouth can spread throughout the body and create one

very sick kitty. Also, mouth discomfort may prevent Kitty from eating properly—or at all. If Kitty drools, stands over her food dish looking like she's interested but won't eat, or goes up to the dish, walks away, returns and continues to repeat the process, her dental problems may already be serious. Brushing Kitty's teeth may sound funny but it's quite the opposite. It is a very important part of Kitty's health-insurance plan.

YOU COULD BE
KILLING YOUR CAT

Take a few minutes and crawl around the floor. See the world from Kitty's perspective. Check out what could harm him. If you do, I bet you'll notice a few things you never considered before. Extension cords dangling from outlets look inviting to kitties who love to play with string. Those Dieffenbachia plants are appealing, too. There are dozens of ways even the most caring owners can harm their cats. Let common sense be your guide. When dealing with Kitty, don't look at a situation and decide what's right. Take a good hard look at anything that's a part of Kitty's life and ask yourself what's wrong. If you can't find something hazardous to Kitty, you're probably not looking hard enough.

Don't leave sharp items lying on countertops or in the sink. When curious Kitty jumps up to investigate he could slice his paws. Of course, be careful with knives but don't forget about razors or scissors.

Where do you store household cleaners and poisons? I bet there are a lot of these products tucked away under the kitchen sink or on shelves Kitty can reach. It doesn't take much to kill a cat. Keep your dangerous household products out of Kitty's reach or at least install childproof locks. I've decided not to relay the gruesome details of what happened to one pet's taste test of a chemical drain opener. What that substance did to the mouth, throat, and stomach of that poor little tyke is more than you'd like to know.

There's usually one member of every family who's taking some form of prescribed medication. Where's the bottle kept? Too often it is left on a nightstand or kitchen table—all within Kitty's reach.

Are there bones in the garbage? Can Kitty raid the pail? Even a small bone lodged in just the right position can kill Kitty. Of course, never give him bones to chew, either.

Did you know that your loose change could be killing Kitty? Pennies minted after 1982 contain a high zinc content. If your cat's stomach acid eats away at the zinc, Kitty could be poisoned.

When spring and summertime roll around, are you guilty of spreading chemicals and fertilizers on your lawn, and then allowing Kitty or other neighborhood animals to walk on it? If Kitty gets a little on his paws and licks it off, he could become quite ill. If he ingests enough of it, he could die.

Don't give aspirin to your cat unless the vet advises it. Aspirin can be toxic for cats.

Antifreeze can be a serious problem. Its sweet taste actually attracts animals. I think you can guess the result by now.

Lots and lots of plants, flowers, and shrubs are dangerous to cats. A little nibble is often all it takes. The list of potentially dangerous greenery is very lengthy. Be sure to check with your local plant nursery about them.

Keep Kitty's safety in mind during the holidays. Decorations mean big trouble for cats. Christmas trees get knocked down (always tie the tree onto something sturdy) and extra extension cords get chewed. Decorative candles tip over and tinsel gets stuck in throats. Glass decorations shatter on the floor and paws get cut. Turkey bones are in abundance. On the Fourth of July there is company running in and out—open doors are an open invitation to a curious Kitty.

Never feed dog food to cats—it's deficient for a cat's nutritional needs.

We all know cats can't fly (except on planes). Why, then, do so many cats end up splattered on the ground, adding to the statistics of high-rise syndrome (cats jumping out of tall buildings). Keep screens or protective bars that Kitty can't squeeze through on all open windows.

Again, never leave Kitty unattended in the car. Cars heat up fast and Kitty could bake (or die) in no time. And as I said before, in cold temperatures automobiles can rapidly turn into iceboxes.

Owners who do not recognize Kitty's need for veterinary attention greatly endanger their pet's health and welfare. Simple items such as yearly physical exams and routine vaccinations are frequently delayed or overlooked completely. Many ailments and life threatening diseases are preventable only if Kitty sees the doctor on schedule.

Also, be alert for signs of Kitty straining when using the litter box or urine that contains blood. Feline urological syndrome (FUS) is an important disease of the urinary system and although it's most often associated with males, FUS can occur in female cats as well. When suspected, FUS should be treated as a life or death medical emergency.

Check for Kitty before starting the laundry dryer. Because dryers are so comfy and toasty, some cats find them a perfect place to take a snooze.

Garden tools have sharp points that can easily puncture tender little cat feet or even poke out an eye.

Great smelling odors filter off the barbecue. If cookouts are part of your life-style, make sure Kitty doesn't make an unexpected leap onto the grill.

If a fireplace or wood-burning stove graces your home, be sure there's enough protective screening surrounding it so Kitty's curiosity doesn't translate to singed paws and hair.

When cold weather strikes, bang on the hood of your car

before starting it. Neighborhood kitties and other small animals sometimes crawl up under the hood to get warm. Give them time to get out.

Many cats don't care for chocolate, but if your Kitty is a chocoholic, watch out. The theobromine in chocolate could be dangerous. Be extra careful around Halloween.

Stroll through the basement, garage, and shed. I bet there are lots of dangerous items. Don't fool yourself into thinking that Kitty is safe because he isn't allowed in those areas. It only takes one time!

ANTICIPATE

Be a responsible owner. Try to prevent any possible tragedy. Any checklist could never contain everything that might harm Kitty. Look, look, look, and look again at everything around your home. Are you sure you're not jeopardizing the safety and even the life of your special pet pal?

KITTY'S DIET
AND NUTRITION

Kitty can select from dry food, canned food, semi-moist food, table food, high ash, low ash, high magnesium, low magnesium, all natural, food coloring, chemical preservatives, vegetable protein, animal protein, high calorie, or low calorie, no tuna, and much, much more.

Have you strolled down the pet-food aisle at the supermarket recently? *Help!* Just how is a cat owner supposed to know what's best?

It's a hard question to answer. Fortunately, pet-food manufacturers are taking diet and nutrition more seriously than ever before. Many vets are also hopping on the bandwagon. The only problem is that pet nutrition was in the dark ages for so long that it's probably going to be a long time before we have all the necessary information. Now, I don't want this to sound like the vets and pet-food companies didn't care. I don't believe that was the case. Quite the contrary, millions of dollars have been poured into research to develop good products. It's just that the idea that good nutrition leads to good health and prevents disease wasn't as strongly followed—even by people—until relatively recently.

I think almost any suggestion I make may be outdated by the time the next batch of studies come in—and even those will be quickly modified with the results of subsequent findings. Check with your vet, read labels (not hype!), and use common sense.

STAY EDUCATED

Most pet-food companies have customer service representatives who will answer your questions and send you literature about their products. Keep informed. Call them frequently. Nudge them. I'm a firm believer in the old saying: the squeaky wheel gets fixed.

Be sure your vet takes diet and nutrition seriously. If he or she gives your questions on nutrition the once-over, find another vet. An animal can only be as strong and healthy as what goes into his or her body. Deficiencies are bound to cause problems.

Inquire about the possibility of FUS (feline urological syndrome). Many vets want cats with this disease put on a special diet.

Kittens, older cats, fat cats, and cats with heart and kidney problems, among others, may benefit from dietary adjustments. Be sure to review this thoroughly with Kitty's doc. Don't just tag along on the conversation, be assertive. Take charge if you have to. Be sure both you and the vet give diet and nutrition the attention they deserve.

VARIETY IS THE SPICE OF LIFE

Variety may be the best insurance for Kitty's eating a healthy, balanced diet. Cats who eat only one type of food day in and day out, all year long, become totally dependent that a given food is balanced and nutritious. If Kitty's tummy can tolerate it, give her different flavors three or four times a week.

WHEN I'M EATING AND KITTY LOOKS UP AT ME, I JUST *HAVE* TO GIVE IN

As a recognized pet expert I'm *supposed* to say, "Never give Kitty table scraps!" But as a cat owner, of course I give Mowdy scraps. He wouldn't let me live in peace unless I did. The key here is moderation. A little bit here and there added into a balanced diet won't hurt. Use common sense and stay away from spicy and fatty foods. When those big eyes look up and plead "feed me," don't feel too guilty about giving in. Just don't go overboard.

FAT CATS/SKINNY CATS

Please don't allow Kitty to gain those extra pounds. It's not good for him. Have the vet check him and then, if he's healthy, feed him less (but in several small meals). Increase his exercise. Be sure Kitty's doc knows about any reducing program you have planned. The vet may have certain suggestions or certain limitations in mind.

On the other hand, if Kitty's weight seems okay but you're worried he's not eating enough, stop worrying! Obviously, Kitty's eating sufficiently for his metabolic rate.

As a general rule of thumb, you can get an idea if Kitty's poundage is too much or too little by feeling her ribs. You should be able to feel just the outline of the ribs. They shouldn't protrude nor should they be buried under layers of fat.

If Kitty's really too thin and you're worried about it, make sure he's healthy. If the vet says everything's in order, try feeding him five, six, or even seven small meals each day. It's a bit of extra work; however, some cats just aren't interested in large meals. Some prefer to nibble and nosh on fresh food rather than food that's been sitting around for an hour or two.

IS KITTY DRINKING?

Many cats don't drink enough water and this can lead to a variety of medical problems. Add some water to Kitty's canned food and make it soupy so she laps it up. Milk in moderation is okay, but it can upset some cats' stomachs. Another possibility is adding a bit of milk to the water to make it more appealing.

DON'T SHORTCHANGE THE VALUE OF DIET

Keeping Kitty on a proper diet is the single most important thing you can do to help ensure that he remains healthy, loving, bright-eyed and bushy tailed.

KITTY MAKEOVERS

We've all watched makeovers on television, as working women and moms were transformed into glamorous females, or construction workers and executives were turned into handsome and sophisticated hunks. It's not that the basic elements for the transformations weren't there all the time, it's just that we don't always know how to best enhance our personal appearance.

Kitty has the same problem. We're not always aware of her beauty and grooming needs.

KITTY NEEDS A BATH

Why is it that everyone assumes cats don't need to be bathed? Yes, they do spend a lot of time licking and cleaning themselves but that's certainly no substitute for a bath. Now, before you think I've gone too far, just ask any professional cat breeder or cat show judge. You'll find they all agree with me.

EASY STEPS TO ADJUST KITTY TO BATHTIME

Don't just toss Kitty into the water and expect her to enjoy it. Take the time to gradually adjust her to the bathtime experience.

First, decide which sink or tub you're going to use. Place a nonskid rubber mat on the bottom so Kitty can get her footing and feel secure.

When you're ready, put a collar on Kitty so you have something to hold on to. Place her in the sink or tub—without water. Repeat this for a few days or weeks until she seems relaxed. If necessary, place some of her favorite toys or food in with her. Don't expect her to be interested in them on the first few tries.

Put a little warm water (check the temperature carefully) in the bottom of the sink or tub. Not a lot—just enough to wet her toes. Practice this a few more times.

Show Kitty the spray attachment, but don't use it yet.

Once nothing's scaring her, spray a little water out of the attachment, pointing it away from her until you're sure she's not afraid of it.

IT'S BATHTIME!

Bathe Kitty early in the day so he isn't damp at bedtime. Wait for a warm day or make sure your home is nice and toasty.

Brush him well to remove all loose, dead hair. A good cat brush is essential. Brush in the direction of as well as against the coat. Also, brush to the skin, not just the top layer of hair. Rub a damp washcloth over the cat, again in the direction of and against the coat. It will help remove even more loose hair.

Put a cotton ball moistened with a little mineral oil in each of Kitty's ears. This will help prevent water from entering the ear area. If Kitty's not thrilled about this cotton ball stuff, practice doing it outside of the sink or tub until he accepts it.

Some people advise using a drop of mineral oil around the

eyes to lessen any irritation caused by shampoo or water in the eyes.

Shampoo Kitty with a cat shampoo. There are dozens on the market, so select a tearless variety, if possibie. If Kitty has dry skin or fleas, be sure to select the appropriate shampoo. Read all the directions carefully. Rinse thoroughly.

Shampoo and rinse a second time if Kitty's bath was really overdue.

Always towel-dry your cat thoroughly. If you can get him adjusted to a hair dryer, all the better. Let him get used to seeing the dryer when it's not operating and then let him adjust to it when it's blowing in the distance. Gradually close the distance between him and the dryer. Be sure the dryer's temperature is low to medium. Don't let it get too hot!

Brush him a little bit here and there while he's drying.

And there you have it—one very clean kitty!

TRICKS OF THE GROOMING TRADE
When Kitty's in between baths, try brushing a little cornstarch through her coat. It's the perfect dry shampoo.

If Kitty's light-colored fur is stained, apply a lemon juice and water spray to the stain. Allow it to sit on the hair before bathing. The lemon juice may very well remove or lighten the stain.

KITTY'S MANICURE
(OR SHOULD I SAY PEDICURE?)
Clipping a cat's nails is probably the one thing about cat ownership that frightens most people. No need for that fear! Once Kitty is comfortable with being touched (see chapter on Kitty Massage), nail clipping is easy. There's one simple trick—just clip the very ends of the tips of the nails. Don't try to take too much off in one sitting. Clip only the tips. Wait a few weeks and clip just the tips again. The vein that everyone's afraid of

cutting will recede during that two-week waiting period. Try to locate the vein before you clip—on some nails you can actually see where it ends.

Use a nail clipper made specifically for cats and have a blood-stopping product on hand just in case you clip the nails too short. Products are available at the pet shop specifically for this purpose. Don't feel too bad if you make the nail bleed. Yes, it does hurt Kitty—the way it hurts if you break your nail below the quick. It stings, sure, but you certainly survive. Everyone, including veterinarians and professional cat groomers, will occasionally cut a nail too short. If it happens to you, at least you know you're in good company.

There's one big advantage to being Kitty's manicurist—you can keep the nails in good shape and at the right length. When Kitty's nails are long, the vet or groomer can cut them back only so far—the quick in the nail needs time to recede. The end result is that Kitty's nails are still too long. Unless you return repeatedly for nail clipping they'll never get trimmed to the proper length.

Do it with the vet or groomer the first time to be sure you understand the process. Just be brave!

WHY IT'S IMPORTANT TO GIVE
THOSE EARS A SNIFF

Infected ears frequently create an odor you can smell. Okay, so you have to stick your nose in Kitty's ears, but early detection of an ear problem makes it worthwhile. Of course, see Kitty's doc if you suspect anything is amiss.

For general cleaning purposes, use a little mineral oil on a cotton ball and swab only the outer parts of the inside of the ear. Don't go too deep—you could injure the little furball's ear.

If there's excessive hair growth around the outer edges of the inside part of the ear, and it's collecting all sorts of dirt and gunk, trim it back carefully. But, please: no scissors in the ear.

FLEAS

Oh no, Kitty has fleas and we're all scratching. Well, get the jump on fleas (and ticks) before they get the jump on you. That's the important step. Don't wait until fleas take over your home before you get into action. And with the tick-related spread of Lyme disease, now more than ever before owners need to be concerned about these parasites as well.

Everyone has a favorite flea and tick approach. There are flea collars, shampoos, dips, sprays, or powders. Whichever you use, be sure to read the directions carefully. If you're using a chemical, make sure you don't misuse the product. If you use too much or if you use it on a very young or old cat, it may make him ill. It may even kill him—so be careful!

The one big step that many people forget about is treating the home environment. Getting the fleas off Kitty is of no help if they are in the carpet and furniture, too. They'll find Kitty again. And again and again. If you need to, call in an exterminator or pack up all living creatures and set off a flea bomb or defogger (available at pet shops and most hardware stores). You may need more than one bomb, depending on the square footage of your home. Again, read the directions carefully. You'll probably need to cover counters and put away food products. Leave home for the suggested period of time. Here again, you're dealing with chemicals, so be a careful consumer.

Vacuum well, including the furniture and all nooks and crannies, and immediately throw out the bag or empty the container in the outside trash.

If your home is flea infested you may have to repeat the process in a week or two, depending on the manufacturer's suggestion.

THE NATURAL APPROACH

Over the years there has been much evidence that certain natural products work against fleas. Unfortunately, some of them have recently been found to create other problems for Kitty. If you're thinking about a natural approach to fleas, check with your vet or a vet specializing in holistic medicine. See what the most recent studies might have to say about whatever substance you're planning to use.

WHAT A GORGEOUS KITTY!

When you're all done, just watch Kitty strut her stuff. She feels better and she knows she looks better. Think I'm kidding? Give it a whirl. Find out for yourself. Kitty will tell you the truth after her makeover.

THE HEIMLICH MANEUVER

If you walked into a room and found Kitty choking, would you know what to do? If you're like most owners you may not have the slightest idea of what needs to be done to save your cat's life. Well, you've probably heard of the Heimlich maneuver for people who are choking—but did you know there's a similar procedure for Kitty? All owners should know how to perform this simple maneuver. Be prepared to step in and, hopefully, ward off a disaster if an unsuspecting Kitty puts something in her mouth that shouldn't be there or simply chokes on some food.

IF KITTY IS CHOKING

Open her mouth and see if the object can be removed from her throat. If it can, simply reach in with your finger and pull it out.

If Kitty is conscious, there is no guarantee you might not be bitten or scratched. Personally, when my animals are in trouble I really don't care about a bite or a scratch. I just do what has to be done to save a life.

In the case of thread, try to recall if there might have been a needle on it. Some experts believe the thread is better left in place and used as an aid to locate the needle.

THE HEIMLICH MANEUVER:
HOW TO GIVE "THE HUG OF LIFE"

Remain as calm as possible.

Place Kitty on his side on a hard surface.

Locate the last rib. (Have a vet show you where it is if necessary.)

Place both hands just behind the last rib.

Press down with a fast and firm motion. Have the vet show you how hard to push down.

Try to move your hands slightly forward as you press down.

Quickly release the pressure from the hands.

Repeat several times in quick succession.

Open the mouth and see if you can retrieve the object from Kitty's throat. If other people are present, continue compressing the chest while someone else tries to remove the object from the throat.

Contact a veterinarian immediately, even if Kitty seems fine.

Always review any first-aid procedure with Kitty's veterinarian. Please do yourself, Kitty, and me a favor. Put down this book and call the vet *now*. Set up a ten-minute appointment in order to review this life-saving procedure. It may turn out to be the best thing you could ever do for your cat!

GETTING A SECOND
OPINION

If there's anything serious going on with Kitty's health, be sure to speak to more than one veterinarian. Pet owners are frequently loyal to their pet's doctor to a fault, not wanting to offend the vet by seeing someone else. Well, most vets are extremely professional and would not hold it against you if you were to seek out another opinion. In fact, many encourage it. If Kitty's vet becomes annoyed because you want to get a second opinion, it's time to get rid of the doctor. Kitty is a member of the family. If any other member of the family was ill and the doctor's advice wasn't adding up, wouldn't you seek out another doctor? You bet you would. Do the same for the little furball. It's only fair.

WHEN TO GET A SECOND OPINION

Anytime surgery is suggested.

Anytime Kitty is being treated for something that isn't clearing up according to the vet's recommendations.

Anytime you have that feeling in the pit of your stomach that things just aren't right or the vet's advice doesn't seem to make sense. Trust your instincts.

WHO SHOULD GIVE A SECOND OPINION

This section should really be entitled "Who *Shouldn't* Give a Second Opinion." Second opinions should never come from anyone in practice with Kitty's doctor or anyone Kitty's doctor recommends or knows too well. I'm not suggesting that, together, they would plan to cheat you. It's just that sometimes people who work closely with each other see things the same way. You want a fresh opinion.

WHAT ABOUT A SPECIALIST?

Absolutely see a specialist if you're dealing with a medical specialty. There are veterinarians who specialize in allergies, cancer, heart problems, and just about anything else. Some doctors even restrict their practices to cats only.

If you're having trouble getting a recommendation for a specialist, contact the Veterinary Medical Association in your county or state. They're often listed in the telephone directory. The reference desk at the public library may also have a listing for the association closest to you.

WHAT IF I DON'T AGREE WITH THE
SECOND OPINION?

It's not uncommon for owners to be dissatisfied with a second opinion. If you have the slightest doubt about what's being suggested, by all means get a third or even fourth opinion. I'm not suggesting you throw out your money and continue looking for a doctor until you find one who tells you what you *want* to hear. What I am saying is: Many times owners know best. They may not be trained in the medical sciences but they do know their cats. Sometimes their sneaky suspicions are more correct than any diagnosis.

Let your heart, brain, and instinct be your guides.

HOLISTIC MEDICINE,
ACUPUNCTURE, AND
CHIROPRACTIC

There are many great things now taking place in veterinary medicine. I strongly suggest that all pet owners stay abreast of new trends in medicine. Sometimes medical practitioners are like wheelbarrows—they're useful tools but they need to be pushed. That's not to say veterinarians are incompetent or ineffective. It simply means that, very often, educated owners can bring out the best in a vet. Let your doctor know that you're on top of what's going on.

And what is going on is very exciting. New areas of medicine (they're not really so new—they've just been pooh-poohed up to now by a lot of health care professionals) are becoming much more widely accepted. Many pets are reaping the benefits of a different way of thinking.

Traditional medicine is still of primary importance to me, but I firmly believe that there are times when other forms of medicine may complement the conventional route.

HOLISTIC MEDICINE

The word is *holistic*, defined as whole, overall. Veterinarians who practice holistic medicine try to treat the entire pet, not just illnesses as they arise. These veterinarians believe that to most successfully treat pets, every factor in their lives must be taken into consideration—nutrition, exercise, home environment, daily stress, even the psychological makeup of the human family members. Based on what we know about the human animal's need for balancing all these things, it's a very interesting idea. Many pet owners believe in this concept to one degree or another. The lack of a total veterinary approach has been a major complaint of many pet owners about the medical community but, of late, there appears to have been a reversal. Now we hear the word holistic more often than ever before and we hear it in the context of our pets.

Holistic vets often place an emphasis on vitamins, minerals, and diets free of chemicals and preservatives. In times of illness they often prescribe a vitamin/mineral complement to help the healing process or boost Kitty's immune system. Some holistic vets even use herb and plant recipes. Before you disregard this as some sort of black magic, remember that many traditional human medications are derived from plants, roots, herbs, and the like.

ACUPUNCTURE

The Eastern art of acupuncture was frowned upon by Western medicine for centuries. But it seems its time has come. Acupuncture makes use of needles that are pushed into certain sensory pathways under the skin to open up the pathways and heal other areas. Acupuncture is generally accepted now, although sometimes unwillingly, by the veterinary community. Many of the world's leading veterinary colleges and hospitals now lend credibility to this ancient medical form.

CHIROPRACTIC

Chiropractic is now more widely accepted for people than ever before. Years ago, chiropractors had all they could do to remain free from being labeled as quacks. Today, it's not uncommon for medical doctors to refer their patients to chiropractors. Often, insurance carriers even cover the costs. Things certainly have changed in the chiropractic field. It's not surprising that many of the same benefits derived for people can be had with pets. However, there are only a few veterinarians trained in chiropractic. Instead, there are chiropractors for people who work on pets as well. For a very well-educated chiropractor who has thoroughly studied Kitty's anatomy working under the supervision of a licensed vet, the lack of a veterinary degree may be acceptable. My fear, however, is that a chiropractor may jump into the animal field without a solid background in the anatomy of the domestic pet.

CHOOSE CAREFULLY

We're lucky there are veterinarians and other trained medical personnel specializing in holistic medicine, acupuncture, and chiropractic. Many have excellent reputations. However, as with any up-and-coming trend, watch out for specialists who make less than common sense. Pay attention to new trends in veterinary care. They more than likely will have a lot to do with Kitty's future—but watch out for the quacks.

SENIOR-CITIZEN CATS
NEED SPECIAL CARE:
WHAT YOU CAN DO TO EXTEND YOUR PET'S
LIFE

It's easy to know when our little kitties are getting older. Either we notice it on the calendar or we become aware of bellies drooping closer to the floor. Or once-active cats are sneaking off for a few extra naps in the sun.

As our pals grow into their golden years, lots of things start to happen. Some are inevitable. Although old age brings irreversible changes to the body and, sometimes, to the behavior, it's a very individual thing. Each kitty has his or her own biological clock. While many cats live from ten to fifteen years, there are more than a few that live beyond twenty. Much has to do with the luck of the draw—good genes. The rest is due to the life-style and environment provided by the owner.

Problems occur when owners don't pay attention to the cat's signs of aging. I think it's because we don't want to consciously acknowledge sweet Kitty is getting on in years. We sort of pretend she is immortal and that the final day will never come.

On the other hand, some owners believe there are seasons of life and that when a pet is in the fall and winter of its years, you must simply accept the things you cannot change. In my opinion, nothing could be further from the truth! There are plenty of ways your cat can be helped through her years of old age. By giving Kitty special senior-citizen care you might very well end up extending her life, adding both quality and quantity to the golden years.

NEXT PATIENT, PLEASE

The easiest thing you can do, the most important thing you must do, and the one thing that is most often not done is to arrange for senior Kitty to see the veterinarian regularly. For old-timers, regularly means more than once a year. Make at least two trips a year, preferably three or four. Help nip old-age problems in the bud. Be sure you're dealing with a vet who understands the importance of preventive medicine with the geriatric cat. Don't allow any quick once-over exams and a declaration that Kitty's fit until the next appointment.

Kidneys are often the first major organ to deteriorate, so be sure Kitty gets a simple blood test for kidney function during each visit. Since the kidneys are the body's filtering system, any slowdown should be noted as soon as it happens. Preventive steps can be taken before a fatal shutdown.

Inquire about changing the cat's diet. Age-weakened body organs don't always process food the way they should. Dietary adjustments can definitely lengthen senior Kitty's life and keep her healthy through her golden years.

You might also want to discuss with the vet the possibility of placing your graying kitty on a vitamin supplement. Although I don't believe in megadoses of vitamins for any animal, I like to place seniors on a dose of an old-fashioned multivitamin/ mineral supplement. Their systems don't always work the way they used to; and eating habits sometimes get a little iffy as they grow older. I believe a good multivitamin/mineral is sort of like chicken soup when you're sick—it might not help but it couldn't hurt. Your vet may have a different opinion, particularly if certain diseases have surfaced, so be sure to speak to the doctor about your cat's vitamin and mineral needs.

Stay alert for dental problems with your geriatric kitty. Infections could be very debilitating at her age.

Be alert to Kitty seeking out warm places to stay. Sure, almost all cats love to snooze in the sun or hang out where the warm air blows from under the refrigerator, but if those four feet seem to be spending more than the usual amounts of time seeking warmth, speak to the vet right away. Her internal thermostat may need adjusting.

NOT TOO SKINNY, NOT TOO PLUMP
—BUT JUST RIGHT

Sometimes old stomachs can't tolerate as much food as they used to in one sitting. Break up senior Kitty's food into smaller meals served more frequently during the day and evening. Some old-timers prefer a little nibble and nosh here and there rather than a couple of big dinners. Keep a careful watch for weight loss—that could be a real sign of trouble ahead. Weigh your old-timer once a week (a simple trick: Weigh yourself first then weigh yourself again with the cat. Subtract the difference and you have Kitty's weight). Remember that the loss of one pound or even half a pound for a small cat could be worth looking into.

Cats with chubby tummies need to lose weight, but don't confuse them with senior kitties experiencing the sagging muscles and droopy bellies of old age.

Older cats don't always drink enough water. It's extremely important to encourage water intake—Kitty has to flush out her system. Add water into some of the meals; many cats will eat their food after they've enjoyed lapping up the soupy mixture created by water and canned food. If, on the other hand, your old pal has shown an increased interest in water, check with the vet right away. Increased thirst could be a symptom of a yet undiscovered problem, like diabetes.

Stay alert to changes in hearing and eyesight. Older cats often experience a decrease in these senses. Vision loss sometimes demonstrates itself by cats pausing or stopping dead in their tracks when they enter a room or when there's been a change in the light. You'll notice Kitty is just kind of standing there, sizing things up before moving around. Of course, if things have gone from bad to worse, you'll notice senior Kitty bumping into things, particularly things not in their normal places.

Hearing loss is a little easier to preliminarily test at home. When Kitty's unaware you're standing behind him, clap your hands or bang a metal spoon on a metal pot, beginning with the lowest possible noise level. If Kitty doesn't respond, increase the volume gradually until you find the point that it's heard. .

Have you noticed Kitty is doing a lot more meowing? Sometimes senior kitties who suffer a hearing loss meow more than they ever did before. It's not just that they've become more vocal overnight, they simply can't hear themselves the way they used to when they were kids.

If loss of vision or hearing is taking its toll on your older furball, don't despair. Most cats adjust surprisingly well to their disabilities. Give senior Kitty a little time—you'll be surprised at how well he'll do.

LUMPS AND BUMPS

Although cancer in cats, particularly older ones, is a serious concern, don't panic over every little lump and bump that shows up. Many of them don't mean anything. However, be sure the vet sees each one. If it is cancer, there are so many medical approaches today that the outcome isn't always as grim as you may think.

OOPS—MISSED THE BOX AGAIN!

If all of a sudden your perfectly house-trained cat is soiling in unexpected places, don't be too tough on the little old puddle-maker. There's a real possibility that Kitty's losing a bit of control and he just can't make it back to the box in time. For Kitty's convenience you might want to add another litter box or two, depending on the size of your home. Place a box on every level the cat patrols. If senior Kitty is upstairs when the urge suddenly hits, he may not be able to make the mad dash down two flights of stairs to the basement. As upset as you might be, I guarantee your once thoroughly trained cat doesn't feel too good about himself either. Embarrassment and humiliation are bound to set in and take their toll on Kitty's emotional well-being before too long.

If accidents remain a problem, or if you find mistakes just outside the box, try to find a litter box with lower sides. Sometimes the golden-year kitty can't make the climb into the box. You might even have to be creative and design a makeshift box with lower lips on the sides. Yes, it will probably mean more litter will get kicked up and tracked onto your floor, but it might save you from cleaning even more offensive substances off the floor. More important, it may save Kitty's pride from being trampled.

Senior kitties allowed to go outdoors for elimination purposes should also have a litter box placed inside, somewhere near their normal exit door. It may come in handy if Kitty can't quite make it through the night anymore. It will also offer you the opportunity to see any problems developing with the stool or urine. Will an outside kitty all of a sudden use an indoor litter box? Probably—even old-timers can learn new tricks. Most cats who are used to staying clean are pretty good about looking for the right alternative when the time comes. If the concept seems too foreign to senior Kitty and soiling remains a problem, refer back to the section on litter box training (starting on page 95) for some quick tips.

Stay alert to variations in elimination habits. A change in the number or consistency of bowel movements could be a red flag signaling a medical problem. Diarrhea is always a possible danger signal. *Never* let it go on without talking to the vet—it can quickly debilitate any cat, particularly a senior kitty. At the other end of the spectrum, some of the old-timers may need the help of a stool softener for constipation. Your vet can guide you to the best selection. Also note Kitty's urination habits. Be sure the cat is urinating freely, not too much more or less than what's been normal over the years.

EMOTIONAL AIDS
TO KEEP THE OLDER CAT
FEELING YOUNG

IT'S PARTY TIME
Throw a party for senior Kitty. Nothing will perk up a senior faster than a festive occasion held in her honor.

SENIOR KITTY PLAYLAND

Don't forget about bringing home new toys and playthings for our special golden-age pal. Sure, I know you're thinking he hasn't played with anything in years but, on the other hand, I bet you haven't brought much of anything home in years, either. Maybe you tried a few things here and there and, at best, there might have been an occasional playful outburst. The key is to keep the playthings rolling in—hoping that one of the games or toys might be just the right one to spark some interest. At the very least, Kitty will like having them around even if they are of no real use. Think of it as the "junk" Grandma collects from the grandkids. There's no way she's going to use those shell ashtrays or plastic-woven key chains, but she sure loves to get and look at them. They're an expression of love. It's nice to know you've been remembered.

AN OLD-TIMER'S MASSAGE

Old bones and muscles might love a little kitty massage. (See chapter on Massage.) We all get a little stiff and sometimes arthritic as the years roll on. A gentle rubdown can be one of the nicest gifts for senior Kitty.

SENIOR KITTIES NEED MAKEOVERS, TOO!

Help out with the grooming. Those old bones don't always allow Kitty to get into the acrobatic grooming positions that young whippersnappers can maneuver. There's nothing worse than feeling unkempt. Believe me, a cat who used to be well-groomed knows the difference. Depression and that old-age lethargy can easily take hold of Kitty's psyche.

While you're doing the extra brushing, check the length of the toenails. Owners sometimes get a little sloppy about toenail length with older cats. Long nails can aggravate old bones and arthritis by forcing Kitty to stand improperly and to incorrectly displace body weight.

FACE-TO-FACE LOVING

Sometimes we take Kitty for granted. Golden Kitty's been around for so long she's become part of the same old routine. So be sure you spend plenty of time with her on the floor, at eye level. Set aside some special time just for this purpose. If Kitty's been allowed on the furniture all these years, you might start to realize that in her older age she's not making the jump up as often as she used to. She may really be missing that extra contact with you she once enjoyed so much.

THINK ABOUT A NEW KITTY KID

Sometimes the best thing you can do for a golden-age cat is to bring a new bouncy furball into the house. The increased activity a kitty kid brings into a home may be the best prescription for adding life to your old-timer. If the two get along famously, that's great. If they don't, because the little kid constantly annoys senior Kitty, that's good too, believe it or not. Even if old Kitty is forced to spend most of her time ducking the nippy kitty, that's probably a whole lot more activity than she had before. Odds are, sooner or later, they will become best buddies.

I know you're concerned you'll be putting your beloved old cat's nose out of joint by bringing in the competition. That may be true. But it will more than likely work itself out. The benefits of a more active life-style generally far outweigh the disadvantages.

BE A TRUE-BLUE FRIEND

Make sure you're very good to senior Kitty. He may be a little crotchety. Maybe he's a bit stiff and feeble. But Kitty's been good to you for a long, long time. He's made you smile and comforted you when you cried. Don't get sloppy about our special friend's care when he needs you most. You'll never forgive yourself if you do. Your loving little pal deserves the best, particularly while the sun is setting on his time on earth.

9

❀　❀　❀

THE FINAL GOOD-BYE

WHEN IT'S TIME TO
SAY GOOD-BYE

One of the most difficult moments for any cat lover is saying the final good-bye to precious Kitty. I don't think it ever gets any easier, no matter how many cats you've had or how many times you have to go through it.

Knowing when to put that little furball to sleep is an incredibly hard decision to make. Sometimes the choice is made for us—Kitty simply falls asleep one night and doesn't wake up in the morning. When death comes to a resting kitty, we can at least take consolation in knowing that it was painless and that Kitty died with dignity.

If Kitty's been battling illness or the effects of old age it's so very hard to know when it's the right time to take the last trip to the doctor. Here again the important word is dignity. I always let that be my guiding light. I want all my pets to spend their remaining days with their dignity intact, enjoying some quality of life. Once I know that's no longer possible, it's easier to come to terms with doing what I must. It's what I'd want for myself. It's the least I can do for Kitty.

Make your own decision when you think the time has come. Don't let others convince you. You'll know when the time is right. Kitty asks for only one thing—that you base your decision on what's right for her. Don't extend her time because you just can't bear to see her go. She lived life as a smart and clever little creature. She doesn't want her final days to be any less than that.

Please don't feel foolish if you grieve. You may even need to take off a few days from work. Not everyone will understand your sense of loss over a cat. Their feelings are of no consequence—you know the relationship you had with Kitty was so very special. Grieving is normal and it's healthy. Realize that you're not alone with those feelings. Millions of people have grieved over the loss of their four-footed pals.

If you find the pain too great to bear by yourself, contact your local humane society. Almost every area has a support group to help owners through these difficult times. You'll be able to talk about your feelings and share your stories. You'll remember the times Kitty made you laugh. You'll remember all those funny little antics of hers. You'll remember all the love she gave you, asking nothing in return for herself. And, yes, you'll even manage a smile or two.

So "Good-bye, dear Kitty. No matter how much time passes I'll never forget you. You'll be in my heart, always and forever. I love you."

10

🐾 🐾 🐾

THE NEXT HELLO

WHAT IS THIS ON
MY DOORSTEP?

Just when you think your heart is broken forever and you could never go through the pain of losing another cat, something strange happens. A little adorable ball of fur shows up on your doorstep. So tiny and alone, he can't be more than six weeks old. You know he's desperate for a home.

Don't feel guilty. You won't be replacing Kitty or trying to forget about her. It's just time to go on. Think of it as Kitty's legacy—she left this world so another little kitty could enjoy the special love and companionship you can provide.

So brush up on your kitty communication and stock up on toys and litter. Here comes that little ball of energy. Like a flash, he races through the living room. There he goes again, only now he's scratching on the dining room chairs. *Boom!*—there he is up on the counter with one flying leap. You'd better keep this book around—I think you're going to need it again.

Good luck with the new one! Somehow I know you'll both do just fine.

ABOUT THE AUTHOR

WARREN ECKSTEIN and his late wife, Fay Eckstein, worked with cats and their owners for more than twenty years. Warren Eckstein has appeared frequently on such television programs as *The Today Show*, *Good Morning America*, *Late Night with David Letterman*, *Live with Regis Philbin and Kathie Lee Gifford*, and Disney's *New Mickey Mouse Club*. He hosts his own *Pet Show* radio programs and is also the author of *The Illustrated Cat's Life*, *The Illustrated Dog's Life*, and *How to Get Your Dog to Do What You Want*.